The
Seven Personalities
of Golf

Discover Your Inner Golfer
to Play Your Best Game

DARRIN GEE

• • •

STEWART, TABORI & CHANG

NEW YORK

Published in 2008 by Stewart, Tabori & Chang
An imprint of Harry N. Abrams, Inc.

Library of Congress Cataloging-in-Publication Data
Gee, Darrin.
   The seven personalities of golf : discover your inner golfer to play your best game /
Darrin Gee.
      p. cm.
   ISBN: 978-1-58479-731-9
   1. Golf--Psychological aspects. 2. Personality. I. Title.
GV965.G34 2008
796.352--dc22   2008005315

Editor: Jennifer Levesque
Designer: Pamela Geismar
Production Manager: Jacquie Poirier

The text of this book was composed in Monotype Bell,
with Belizio and Trade Gothic.

Printed and bound in China

10 9 8 7 6 5 4 3 2 1

HNA
harry n. abrams, inc.
a subsidiary of La Martinière Groupe

115 West 18th Street
New York, NY 10011
www.hnabooks.com

Dedicated to my children,
Maya and Eric,
whose beautiful, little personalities
constantly remind me of what's
most important in life.

THE SEVEN PERSONALITIES OF GOLF

The Intimidator

The Swashbuckler

The Methodologist

The Gamesman

The Steady Eddie

The Laid-Back

The Artist

CONTENTS

INTRODUCTION

"My ability to concentrate and work toward that goal has been my greatest asset."

Jack Nicklaus

WHEN some people read the title of this book, their initial response may be "Is this about golfers with multiple personality disorder?" Not quite. It's not about the scientific definition of multiple personality, but rather the many different styles and approaches a golfer might demonstrate on the golf course.

At my Spirit of Golf Academy in Hawaii, I often poll my students asking them to describe their own personality on the golf course. Some say they are apprehensive. Others say they are hyper or fast, while others describe themselves as relaxed or laid back.

Some golfers see themselves as aggressive on the golf course. For every shot, they give it their all, oftentimes leading to huge, monstrous drives, but at the same time, this approach may result in wayward shots out of bounds. If there is a lake guarding a green and they have 235 yards to the hole, they don't lay up. They go for it. Anything less would not feel right. That's a style, approach, or *personality* on the golf course. It's how one carries oneself.

On the other hand, some may be very quiet, steady, and deliberate. They may calculate each and every shot, perhaps evaluating several options and then choosing the one that has the highest probability of success. On a hole with the flag tucked behind a cavernous bunker, this golfer will choose a spot in the middle of the green as the target. Some may call this conservative or cautious. Again, that is a particular style, approach, or personality.

The interesting thing about personalities is that they are multi-faceted. If you were to describe your personality off the golf course, you might come up with one word that summarizes you overall. But at the same time, you will most likely think of several other words that describe the many aspects of who you are. It is important to realize that everyone has aspects of every personality type to a certain degree.

The key is to understand and identify which is your main or *dominant* personality type, understand the strengths and weaknesses of that particular type, and then learn how to maximize those strengths and minimize those weaknesses. In addition, it is just as important to understand the other nondominant or *secondary* personalities and know when to borrow traits from those personalities at key moments on the golf course to help you perform at your best.

For example, a conservative golfer can benefit from taking a more aggressive approach at certain times during a round of golf. Many of these types of players steadily plod their way about the golf course, rarely making a major mistake. They shoot for the middle of the fairway and the fat part of every green. They rarely cut the corner of a dogleg, and if there's water, they shy away. Tucked pins are ignored, and oftentimes, they leave the driver in the bag in favor of a club that gives them a higher chance of hitting a fairway in regulation.

If this player was on the 17th hole in a tournament and was behind by two strokes, he or she would need to borrow from the aggressive personality. Let's assume it's a 185-yard par-3 hole where the pin is located just a few paces from a large lake fronting the green. Normally, this golfer would take a club and shoot for the middle or back of the green. That would get the ball safely on the green and away from the water, but leave him or her with a long attempt at birdie.

Yes, it's possible to make a thirty- or forty-foot putt, but with a much lower probability. This golfer needs to get the ball in the hole or, at the very least, close enough to increase the chances of making birdie. The player must get aggressive in his or her approach and go for the pin. Even though this type of shot, which brings the water into play, goes against the natural tendencies of the conservative golfer, this would be a time when it is warranted. The golfer must go for it to win and play his or her best golf.

This also goes for the player with a risk-taking personality. The "go for it" philosophy does not always serve the golfer well. For example, let's assume that a different player who is a risk taker has a three-stroke lead with two holes to go in a golf tournament and is standing on the same 185-yard par-3 17th hole described above. The risk-taking approach would normally lead the golfer to attempt a shot just over the water and onto the green, setting up a birdie attempt. However, that particular shot brings the lake and potential trouble into play and, if not executed to perfection, could easily end up in the water and subsequently jeopardize the lead and tournament.

This would be a perfect time to borrow a trait or approach from another personality type. An aggressive shot is clearly unnecessary with such a large lead. At moments like this, the aggressive player must recognize that his or her dominant personality is a detriment or liability. He or she must choose strategically from another personality. Perhaps, the golfer can borrow the steady, calculated approach—aim for the middle of the green, thereby taking the water out of play, getting down in two putts, and moving on to the last hole with at worst a one-shot lead.

This philosophy certainly applies to the professional tour player. In the 2006 PGA Championship at Winged Foot Golf Club in New York, Phil Mickelson had a one-stroke lead standing on the tee of the 72nd hole. Par would most likely give him the championship.

However, his aggressive, go-for-broke approach got the best of him. He had hit only two fairways during the final round. Instead of hitting a club that would get him safely in the fairway when he needed it most, he decided to go with his driver. He proceeded to push the ball left, where it bounced off a hospitality tent and into the rough.

His ball was now about two hundred yards from the pin, with trees between him and the green. He had to cut or slice the ball around the trees to reach the elevated green, which was guarded by traps. Again his aggressive golf personality got the best of him. He selected his 3-iron and went for the green. The ball hit the trees and bounced backward, ending up in the rough again. On his third shot, the line to the pin was still blocked by trees. He went for the green again and proceeded to cut the ball into the left greenside bunker. He blasted the next shot from a buried lie in the trap through the hole, and then got up-and-down for a 6. On the last hole of a major championship, he shot a double bogey. He lost the championship by one stroke—a historic collapse.

There were several opportunities during the hole to downplay his dominant go-for-broke personality and adopt another that could have served him better. The tee shot—instead of hitting his driver, which was off all day, he could have been more conservative by hitting a fairway wood or long iron. That would have given him a higher probability of hitting the ball in the fairway. The second shot—instead of trying to slice the ball around the trees and reach the green with what would have been a miraculous shot, he could have punched out to the fairway, giving him great position to hit the next shot close to the hole. It still would have given him the chance to save par and win the championship. Even on the third shot— instead of going for the green, he could have laid up to a spot short of the green and out of the traps, where with his phenomenal short game, he could still have gotten up-and-down for bogey, which, at the very least, would have set up a play-off.

Of course, it's easy to see all of this in hindsight. In fact, for all of us armchair players and coaches, it's always easy to formulate an opinion. The key is, when you are in the heat of battle during a round of golf, you need to learn how to recognize those moments when you must minimize your dominant personality instincts and adopt a more fitting approach in order to achieve a higher level of success.

The seven personalities that are categorized in this book have been chosen as examples that I believe are representative of the majority of golfers. They are not based on a scientific analysis or exhaustive selection of psychological personality types, but rather on my general observations. This means that there are more than just the seven generalized personality types described in this book. Also note that the individuals mentioned as examples of each personality type are not necessarily solely and totally defined as such. In other words, this is all in fun.

After taking the survey at the end of each chapter, you may find yourself identified as a particular personality type that doesn't quite match how you want to view yourself. Please don't take it too seriously. This only indicates that you have a few traits of that particular personality. On the other hand, if you are convinced that your style surely matches a particular personality profile, but the survey indicates otherwise, that does not mean you do not fit that profile per se. It may indicate that while you have certain traits of the profile, you do not demonstrate them all the time.

After taking each survey, you may find that you identify strongly with one particular personality. This is your *dominant* personality. Some may see themselves possessing traits and qualities of several personalities. Don't worry—carrying qualities from different personality types is desirable as long as you learn when and how to use each type in the most effective way. Most golfers will have one dominant personality or style, with traits from several other secondary personality profiles.

This book will help you play your best golf no matter your personality. Each chapter is dedicated to a particular personality type and describes the profile with examples of professional and amateur golfers who demonstrate it. In addition, you will be able to identify your dominant personality and learn more about yourself by using the survey at the end of each chapter, called the Seven Personalities of Golf Profiler, which will help you do the following:

1. Identify your own personality profile

2. Learn how to maximize the strengths and minimize the weaknesses of your dominant personality

3. Learn how and when to borrow traits from every other personality (considered secondary personalities for you) to play your best golf.

The personality profiler is a tool to help you determine who you are and how you play the game of golf. Once you know this, you will be able to determine the best approach and corresponding shots to use at critical moments on the golf course, to help you play to your potential.

OVERVIEW OF THE SEVEN PERSONALITIES OF GOLF

The seven personalities in this book are identified with descriptive words rather than scientific terminology. These seven personalities were selected based on the author's experience working with and coaching thousands of golfers at the Spirit of Golf Academy and through observation and research about past and present professional golfers from around the world.

The golfers, professional and amateur, used as examples have been chosen based on the author's own external observations. People were not interviewed or categorized based on psychological examination. The individuals identified as examples of a particular personality profile are not necessarily this way in actuality, either on or off the golf course. However, this is how they appear to the author when they're playing the game of golf. The following seven personalities represent a cross-section of the golfing world:

1. *THE INTIMIDATOR*

2. *THE SWASHBUCKLER*

3. *THE METHODOLOGIST*

4. *THE GAMESMAN*

5. *THE STEADY EDDIE*

6. *THE LAID-BACK*

7. *THE ARTIST*

Now let's have some fun!

CHAPTER ONE

THE INTIMIDATOR

"Never let up. The more you can win by, the more doubts you put in the other players' minds the next time out."

Sam Snead

THE INTIMIDATOR walks up to the first tee with a certain air. Short on words. A quick, firm, almost bone-crushing handshake. It's all in the body language. The eyes. This person always wins a staring contest. His or her demeanor is all business. There's no time or space for idle chitchat or getting to know you. This golfer has one thing in mind: win.

The Intimidator is the golfer who uses a steely approach to stay focused on his or her own game. Whether intentional or not, this golfer's intimidating style and approach often have a strong effect on an opponent's focus and play. Opponents often self-destruct in the presence of an Intimidator. Physically, there is no difference and nothing has changed. The two golfers are playing the same golf course under the same conditions. The only difference is in how an opponent reacts and responds to the Intimidator's competitive nature. Many golfers allow the energy of an Intimidator to affect their own play adversely.

Look no further for examples of the Intimidator personality profile than two of the greatest players of all time—Tiger Woods and Jack Nicklaus. Their mere presence often puts fear into the eyes of their opponents. Many players give up before they even begin.

Woods's winning percentage, or close ratio, when entering the final round of a tournament with a lead or share of the lead is phenomenal. Of those tournaments, he has won over 90 percent.

Even more revealing is that in the four pressure-filled major championships (Masters, U.S. Open, British Open, PGA Championship), Tiger is a perfect 13 for 13 when entering the final round with the lead or share of the lead. No professional, past or present, even comes close on either ratio.

Many say Tiger just played better than the competition. If you base the results simply on the virtue of score alone, this is true. However, how and why he scored better is far more illuminating. Recognize that his fellow *final group* opponents had been playing great golf and earned their way into the final group. They were tied for first or second going into the last round of each tournament.

Woods's average final-round score when leading or tied for the lead heading into the final round of a major championship is about 69. His playing opponents' final round score average is almost 73. Close to a four-stroke difference! Not only does he win, he wins convincingly.

My conclusion: Tiger's intimidating presence combined with steady play had a dramatic effect on his opponents' ensuing falter and collapse. This led to large differences in score and ultimately to Tiger's victory. In other words, even though his fellow competitors played under the same golf course conditions, they fell prey to Tiger's aura.

The Intimidator has an awesome effect on others. His or her physical presence is surely intimidating. But the expert Intimidator affects others without being in the same physical space or even on the golf course. During Jack Nicklaus's prime, his opponents often admitted they had given up long before teeing up the golf ball. If Jack had a lead, they "knew" that he would never "let" them back into the game. His reputation preceded him, and half the battle was already won. Players were competing for second place.

The Intimidator does not necessarily view intimidation as his or her primary weapon on the golf course. In fact, many intimidators may not even realize how their demeanor affects the play of others. However, they do know that if they stay focused on their game, then others will have to play their best to be competitive. That's a powerful existence. The most impressive aspect of this personality is that if the Intimidator stays focused, plays the best he or she can play, and still loses, this golfer is the first to admit that an opponent played better and deserved the victory.

Being an Intimidator can also have its shortcomings. The natural tendency for a person with this personality type is to be very intense and driven. At times, this can be a detriment. I worked with Michael, a single-digit handicapper, on managing his emotions throughout an entire round of golf. In general, being an Intimidator served him well and helped him play his best golf. As an Intimidator, he clearly had his goals in mind and was aware of his capabilities as a golfer. However, at times, when his opponent hit a longer drive or took a large lead, he became flustered and frustrated.

His competitive nature affected his game adversely. He would swing harder in an attempt to keep up. He would attempt shots that were out of his realm and skill set. His ego would get in the way. He allowed the play of others to affect his game. In these situations, the Intimidator was intimidated. He could not adapt and downplay his own dominant personality.

Intimidators, like Michael, can be too rigid at times. I taught him how to recognize when he was experiencing diminishing returns on his efforts—in other words, the threshold when more effort begot lesser results. If he reaches that point, he must borrow from another personality type to level out his play. Flexibility helps the Intimidator develop a more balanced approach to his or her game and, ultimately, leads to greater success on the golf course.

THE INTIMIDATOR

STRENGTHS	*High level of focus*
	Steady
	Goal-driven
	Wants to play best always
	Blocks out distractions easily

WEAKNESSES	*Rigid*
	Slow to adapt
	Tries too hard
	Difficult to maintain high level of intensity
	Lack of emotional balance
	Overly intense

SEVEN PERSONALITIES OF GOLF PROFILER

Determine if THE INTIMIDATOR personality is your dominant personality by completing the following quiz/survey:

	STRONGLY AGREE	AGREE	NEUTRAL	DISAGREE	STRONGLY DISAGREE
	5	4	3	2	1

1. I am highly focused on the golf course. _____

2. I keep to myself when playing golf. _____

3. I am an intense person on the golf course. _____

4. I thrive on competition. _____

5. I always want to win. _____

6. I play better in groups rather than when alone. _____

7. I play better in groups that are competitive. _____

8. I play best when betting, gambling, or competing on the golf course. _____

9. I don't mind if my opponent plays poorly. _____

10. I enjoy beating my opponent. _____

YOUR TOTAL SCORE *(add up all ten answers)* _____

40–50 DOMINANT PERSONALITY | 30–39 SECONDARY PERSONALITY | <30 NON-PERSONALITY

HOW TO USE
THE INTIMIDATOR
PERSONALITY

DOMINANT PERSONALITY

If the Intimidator is your dominant personality, then you must learn how to best leverage it on the golf course. Always set goals for yourself, whether during a round of golf, a tournament, or even a practice session. For the Intimidator, there must be a purpose to everything. To trigger a higher level of performance, you need to maintain a higher level of intensity than most others.

Competition drives the Intimidator. An external opponent is not always necessary, as internal competition is equally powerful as a motivational factor. The Intimidator is very success- and results-driven. Thus, for every shot, hole, or round of golf, there must be a definitive goal.

If there is nothing "on the line," the Intimidator often loses interest and intensity, which may lead to a lower level of performance. Naturally, playing in a competitive situation brings out the best in his or her game. To create this intensity, the Intimidator should play games such as skins, or make wagers against fellow players.

If the others in your playing group choose not to participate, then you can create pressure by challenging yourself to a match. For example, challenge yourself to

- ••• Shoot more birdies than bogeys in a round
- ••• Hit ten or more fairways and/or fourteen or more greens in a round
- ••• Take less than thirty putts in a round

Make the consequences real and significant, enough to generate a definitive attraction (for the reward) and aversion (to the punishment). If you achieve the goal, you will reward yourself, such as by buying a new club. If you fall short, you must punish yourself, such as by doing some undesirable chore at home. Create a scenario that raises the level of intensity and, subsequently, your game.

On occasion, you may benefit from abandoning your typical competitive approach. This means that for 97 percent of the time, press on. However, for the other 3 percent, balance out your intensity. It is very difficult to maintain the highest level of intensity for an entire round, let alone an entire tournament. Periodically throughout the round, step back and loosen up between shots.

Loosening up can be physical or mental. When you loosen up your body physically by doing stretches, shaking out your arms, or simply moving muscles in a different way (e.g., squatting, bending sideways), it releases excess tension that may have been building up

through repetitive motions such as the golf swing. [1] Once you use a different movement, the body will loosen up overall, allowing for better golf shots.

Likewise, when you take a mental break for just a few moments from long periods of intense concentration and focus, it allows your mind the freedom to relax. As a result, you will think more clearly going forward and make better decisions in shot selection and course management strategy.

Ed was one of the most intense golfers I have ever met. At his best, he was a scratch player who shot in the low 70s and often crept into red num-

1

bers. After some health issues, his game changed significantly and his scores "ballooned" into the mid to high 70s. He was extremely frustrated that his body couldn't produce the same shots as before.

I explained to Ed that one's physical condition changes constantly. Some days you will feel stronger, and other days you will feel less than 100 percent. The key is to adapt and adjust to how your body is responding on that particular day. In other words, even if you are not at 100 percent physically, you can make up for that by being at 100 percent mentally, which includes strategy, course management, shot selection, and managing your emotions.

Ed found that his physical capabilities could no longer match the same level of intensity he'd had before health issues arose. He needed to alter his approach accordingly. Instead of powering every shot, he could be smarter and hit more strategic shots. To increase his physical and mental stamina, he needed to relax more and break up his intensity. I advised him to take a physical and mental break every four holes by stopping and getting a drink of water and/or a snack. That's all. Just a few moments to focus on something other than golf would give Ed the necessary balance before shifting back to his game 100 percent. This helped him level out his intensity, and as a result, he became a better, more balanced golfer.

This type of technique is most effective for the Intimidator when he or she is heading into a critical stage of competition or stretch of challenging holes. Shifting out of the Intimidator personality profile at key moments will help the Intimidator become even more powerful on the golf course.

SECONDARY OR NON-PERSONALITY

If the Intimidator is your secondary personality or non-personality, you can benefit by learning how and when to borrow a few certain traits at critical times on the golf course. There may be a situation or two that call for a more aggressive approach.

Perhaps you have been playing inconsistently of late and have a lot of doubt in your swing and overall game. You play with hesitation and rarely commit fully to your shots, resulting in less than full-effort swings. This is a time when using the Intimidator personality profile can help kick-start your game up a level. Shift your attitude and approach.

Become the Intimidator by focusing on a clear goal, blocking out all distractions, calling the shot, and then going for it without hesitation or reserve. You may have to repeat a few words over and over again in your mind to get your energy and focus in the right direction. For example, repeat to yourself the words "Go for it" or "In the hole" or "Hit the flag."

This situation is similar to an athlete who hits the "wall" or reaches his or her physical limitation and then applies mental focus to continue or even lift his or her performance to another level. Endurance athletes, such as marathoners or triathletes, utilize this type of mental performance technique to break through critical stages of a race when fatigue sets in. If an athlete is unable to get past these hurdles, he or she will see a dramatic decrease in concentration and performance. For some, it will spell the end of their competition. Using the Intimidator personality profile can be as effective as being your own drill sergeant or coach.

The Intimidator personality is also effective for the player who needs to raise his or her level of intensity. Some golfers play with a laid-back, happy-go-lucky style which follows their personality and is conducive to performing at their best. However, there will be times when adopting the Intimidator personality will help them get to the next level.

I recently played in a charity golf tournament in which my group consisted of four players with handicaps/indices of different levels. The tournament format called for the best score (gross and net) from the foursome on each hole to determine the group's overall score. With the handicap system, certain players were allowed extra strokes on the more difficult holes.

One of our players was a 20 handicapper named Craig. He was the most easygoing guy in the group. In fact, he had stepped off a red-eye flight that morning and driven to the golf course, arriving just in time for the tournament. His hair was ruffled, his shorts were wrinkled, and he wore tennis shoes—not your prototypical country club golfer. His appearance was indicative of his personality on the course—just out for a good time and more interested in conversation than score.

2

On one hole, Craig was allowed two extra strokes. If he shot par, or 4, the score would be adjusted to an eagle 2. He managed to hit a good drive to the 140-yard mark. As he prepared to hit his approach shot, he was talking about this and that and appeared to be as unfocused as ever. At that moment, our forecaddie said, "Craig, focus. We need this shot right now. Put your best swing on it."

You could almost observe a complete shift in his demeanor. His body language and facial gestures changed. [2] He immediately became a tour player, stepping back and approaching the shot with purpose. He nailed it and made his par for a net eagle. This is an example of a situation on the golf course when traits from the Intimidator personality can serve a player well. So on occasion, even if the Intimidator is not your dominant personality, borrow this technique and increase your level of play immediately.

CHAPTER TWO

THE SWASHBUCKLER

"The most rewarding things you do in life are often the ones that look like they cannot be done."

Arnold Palmer

WITH the title of Swashbuckler, think of a pirate or cowboy, who swoops in, with grace, style, and an aura of confidence and charisma, to save the day. He or she does this in such a charming way that all those who observe it immediately fall for this person. The public feels this golfer's emotions and experiences, his or her highs and lows. That is perhaps why there is such an affinity for Swashbucklers. We feel they are one of us.

On the golf course, the Swashbuckler seems to thrive on risk and taking chances, even when the probability of success is low. If there is an opening, however small, the Swashbuckler will go for it simply because it exists. These golfers don't weigh the odds and take the option with the lowest amount of risk. They just go for it, sometimes to their own detriment.

When they take risks and succeed, the triumph is shared by all. If they fail, the pain is equally felt, and perhaps even more so. In some ways, observers live vicariously through the Swashbuckler. Because the Swashbucklers wear their hearts on their sleeves, they are universally admired by and endeared to the public. We tend to identify more closely with this type of golfer.

They often possess more natural talent and skill than their peers, but that does not always equate with more victories and successes. They are gamblers in a way. They see the world in black and white. Victory or defeat. No in-between exists.

It is quite typical for a golfer with a Swashbuckler personality to finish first. It is equally possible for this person to finish last. They are not necessarily consistent top-ten finishers. More often than not, they are all or nothing. This quality and approach to golf, and perhaps life, is so appealing to the golf fan. The Swashbuckler demonstrates an unsurpassed love of the game and a flair for excitement, risk, and thrill.

At times, the Swashbuckler applies his or her strengths to create the most amazing shots seen in competition. The Swashbuckler's high-risk, high-reward play is lauded and encouraged by his or her fans. These golfers are often followed by armies or swarms of people. And the groups of followers are diverse—young and old, men and women, seasoned low handicappers as well as non-golfers. The Swashbuckler has universal appeal.

Arnold Palmer fits this description. His "go-for-broke" philosophy combined with his boyish charm, charisma, and cowboy swagger was, and still is, irresistible to fans. Even today, he is arguably the most popular figure in golf, even though he has retired from the professional arena.

Arnold would keep it simple. As his father taught him, he would hit the ball as hard as he could, and then he would hit the ball as hard as he could. This attitude led him to tournament victory after tournament victory. But what set him apart from all the rest was not how many tournaments he won, but rather *how* he won them.

Oftentimes, when he was seemingly all but out of the tournament, he would come from behind with high-octane energy and force. Trailing by seven strokes heading into the final round of the 1960 U.S. Open at Cherry Hills Country Club in Colorado, he boldly grabbed his driver and went for the green on the par-4 313-yard first hole. To the thrill of the crowd, he drove his ball onto the green and set the tone to achieve the greatest final-day comeback in U.S. Open history.

If you ever saw Arnold play golf, you know he rarely held back. His go-for-it philosophy served him well overall. In fact, most golfers who have Swashbuckler personalities play their best when they take risky shots. The thrill and excitement of pulling off a difficult shot is what gets them going.

I believe some of these golfers use the same traits off the golf course. They love and enjoy not only golf, but life as well. Swashbucklers are equally daring, and successful, in their business affairs. They do not necessarily show off their skills or achievements. It is simply who they are. They put all of themselves into every shot and every experience.

However, there are times when this philosophy can be a detriment. This type of individual could benefit from knowing when to tone down the go-for-broke personality. As mentioned in the introduction, Phil Mickelson's experience in the 2006 U.S. Open is an example of the Swashbuckler personality gone awry. He could have benefited from toning down his natural approach and style.

For 99 percent of the time, Phil needs to play his Swashbuckler personality to perform at his best. He said in an interview that he needs to play a high-risk/high-reward game in order to have fun and enjoy golf and ultimately play his best. However, even Phil realized that he had to tone down that approach at times in order to win major championships, which he has done so successfully. If he had applied that philosophy to the 2006 U.S. Open, he would have had one more.

One of my golf academy clients named John was an extremely gifted twenty-five-year-old golfer with a flair for excitement. He called every shot or, in other words, he told me exactly what type of shot he was going to hit before he hit it. "I'm going to hit a high draw, starting out toward that cloud, and then turning about twelve feet to the left," he'd say prior to executing the shot. "Next, I'm going to hit a low-boring four-iron that will stay under the wind and roll forever."

No doubt he had the skills and, more importantly, the confidence and attitude to create the shots he described. However, when I took him on the golf course for a playing lesson, his Swashbuckler personality let him down at times, especially when we reached the 6th hole, a 404-yard par-4 with a large lake to the right of the green. The hole had one lone tree about 130 yards short of the green, fronting the lake. From the tee, the tree appeared to be in the middle of the fairway.

I described the hole and various strategies for playing the hole. If the tee shot went too long and right of center, the tree would block the approach to the green. If the tee shot went left, it would need to carry over 275 yards to fly the sand traps. The safe, high-percentage landing area that would give an unobstructed approach to the green would require less than a driver for John. What did John do?

His Swashbuckler personality got hold of him. He took his driver and attempted to fly the traps on the left, which was a stretch for him. He hit the ball far, with enough distance to clear the traps, but because he felt he had to swing a little harder, his ball faded slightly to the right . . . directly behind the tree.

On the next shot, he was too close to the tree to go over it, and the tree trunk was blocking the line to the green if he attempted to go under. Going to the right would take him over the lake and he would have to hook it at least fifty yards. The safe route would be to punch the ball left into the fairway to set up a third shot from seventy-five yards—a perfect sand wedge for John. What did he do?

Among the tree branches, he saw an opening about the size of a steering wheel. He couldn't help himself and took out an 8-iron. Amazingly, the ball headed right for the opening, but one tiny branch knocked it off line to rattle in the tree and drop into the lake. John was furious. He felt robbed. Now he was looking at double bogey or worse.

He never viewed this as a low-percentage shot per se. It was just a shot, and a fun one at that. The thrill of potentially pulling off the shot got the best of him. This would have been a good time for John to soften his dominant Swashbuckler personality and adapt to the conditions and situation at hand. By applying a more objective perspective instead of going with his initial knee-jerk reaction, John would have been able to make a more thorough evaluation of the risk and reward in each option. More than likely, he would have realized that he could punch out to the fairway, leaving him an unobstructed approach to the green. With his outstanding shot-making skills, he would then have had a high-percentage attempt to get the ball close to the hole, setting up the opportunity to save par.

THE SWASHBUCKLER

STRENGTHS

Fun, easygoing attitude

Never bored

Creative

Fearless

Risk-seeking

WEAKNESSES

Lack of perspective

Excessive

Zones out

SEVEN PERSONALITIES OF GOLF PROFILER

Determine if THE SWASHBUCKLER personality is your dominant personality by completing the following quiz / survey:

	STRONGLY AGREE	AGREE	NEUTRAL	DISAGREE	STRONGLY DISAGREE
	5	4	3	2	1

1. I have a "go for it" attitude. _____

2. I like taking risks on the golf course. _____

3. I have a vivid imagination. _____

4. I consider myself a go-getter on and off the golf course. _____

5. I like to imagine different types of shots from the same lie. _____

6. I enjoy the thrill of attempting and achieving a difficult shot. _____

7. I like playing a golf course for the first time. _____

8. I enjoy courses with many hazards and challenges. _____

9. I enjoy golfing with others rather than by myself. _____

10. I enjoy playing games on the golf course. _____

YOUR TOTAL SCORE *(add up all ten answers)* _____

| 40–50 DOMINANT PERSONALITY | 30–39 SECONDARY PERSONALITY | <30 NON-PERSONALITY |

HOW TO USE THE
SWASHBUCKLER
PERSONALITY

DOMINANT PERSONALITY

If the Swashbuckler is your dominant personality, there are several ways to leverage it most effectively on the golf course. Always view the game of golf as a *game*. While the goal and purpose of a game is to achieve a certain outcome, having fun along the way is just as, if not more, important. So remember to always have fun out there. The moment golf becomes boring or mundane, you must find a way to make it more exciting and enjoyable.

One way is to "call your shots." This is a great way to generate interest and excitement. Instead of hitting the ball with the same swing over and over again, try hitting different types of shots. If you're on the driving range, go for a high draw, followed by a cut, followed by a punch shot, all to the same 125-yard marker. Around the greens, mix up the variety of shots by hitting one high, the next a bump-and-run, and then putting from off the green. By calling and attempting different types of shots, you will keep the game interesting and constantly feed your desire for risks and the thrill you feel when you pull off a shot.

Some golfers with the Swashbuckler personality profile may not feel they have the skills to call and create different types of shots at will as described above. Go for it anyway. You'll have more fun, and to your surprise, you may find you'll be able to hit some of the shots you call.

There will be times when the Swashbuckler personality can be a detriment. In the 1999 British Open, Jean Van de Velde held a three-shot lead with one hole to go in the championship. When interviewed several months after the tournament, he said that his philosophy in golf was to never coast into a victory, but rather to always play the game with full force. This rigid Swashbuckler-like attitude proved to be his demise.

Instead of hitting a tee shot that had a higher probability of landing in the middle of the fairway with a 3-wood or long iron, he teed off with his driver, which he pushed right of the fairway, luckily going over the burn (creek) that meandered down to the hole. He escaped with that mental error. However, on the next shot, instead of laying up to the fairway to set up a short or mid iron to the green, he decided to go for the flag. What made this shot even more daunting was the fact that the green was fronted by the burn and sand traps. Again, the Swashbuckler personality blurred his vision of the big picture. He went for the green and presumably an attempt at a birdie he did not need.

He swiped at the ball with a 2-iron and watched it drift right. The ball cleared the burn in the air but hit the railing of the spectator stands and bounced backward over the burn sixty yards short of the hole. Jean then attempted to hit the next shot in knee-high rough, and it fell woefully short into the burn. At this stage, he was in a bit of shock, which hindered his decision-making even more.

He crazily rolled up his pants and headed into the water. Just as he was preparing to hit the shot, the ball submerged. He was then "forced" to take a drop, which resulted in a penalty shot. He was now hitting his fifth shot. If he could get up and down (i.e., hit the green and one-putt), he could still win the championship. He aimed directly for the flag, tucked behind a large sand trap. The ball fell short into the bunker. He blasted out of the trap, made the putt for a triple-bogey 7, and let out an enormous scream of emotion. Unfortunately, he fell back into a three-way tie and then lost in the play-off.

This is an example of a time *not* to use the Swashbuckler personality. There were several key moments when Jean could have altered his approach. On the tee, he could have shifted his mentality and strategy. Knowing he had a three-stroke lead, all he needed to do was score a bogey or even a double bogey to win. He could have mentally viewed the hole as a par-5. If he shot a 5, his closest opponent would have to shoot an eagle 2 to tie him—highly unlikely on the difficult 18th hole at Carnoustie. This is perhaps not the typical flashy Swashbuckler way to play, but in this case it would have been prudent. On the next shot, he could have punched to the middle of the fairway. As for the pitch shot from the deep rough, he could have actually hit it sideways into the fairway and still had a clear shot to the hole for his fourth. All he needed to do was get on the green and two-putt for the victory. Instead, he went for the pin and hit it in the burn. In the end, the Swashbuckler personality let him down.

SECONDARY OR NON-PERSONALITY

Many golfers play the game more conservatively, opting for high-percentage, safe routes for the majority of their shots. This approach, more often than not, leads these golfers to better shots and lower scores. However, on occasion, borrowing the Swashbuckler personality may help the more conservative golfer take the game to the next level.

For example, if you are a couple strokes behind in a competition with only a few holes left, abandoning your conservative approach and applying the Swashbuckler personality profile may prove useful. Knowing that a birdie can have a large impact on your overall performance, you can change your strategy. Instead of laying up on a par-5, go for the green. On a par-3 with the pin tucked behind a trap or water, instead of going for the fat of the green, add a little flair and take dead aim. [3]

3

When you do this, you will be exiting your comfort zone. That's a good thing. Going outside the box can often trigger performance to a level that you could not have otherwise imagined. Adopting a trait from the Swashbuckler personality profile may be an easier way for you to push yourself to the next level. At times, dramatic shifts are more effective than small, gradual changes in creating a large impact.

By seeing yourself as a more flamboyant player and playing accordingly at critical stages in a round, match, or tournament, you can uplift your energy and shift your game. If you feel bored or unexcited by your round of golf, try something out of the ordinary.

I recently played a round of golf with some friends. One of the guys, Dan, seemed a bit bored and uninterested, not his usual self. He wasn't hitting the ball particularly well and just seemed to be going through the motions. Then we got to the par-three 5th hole, guarded by a lake on the right.

Dan usually aimed to the left side of the hole and let his natural cut or fade bring it back to the middle of the green. However, at this moment when he seemed so down and listless, I told him, "Go for it. Forget about the center of the green, go for the flag!" With that, his whole attitude shifted. Even though the water was now in play and made the shot riskier, Dan adopted the Swashbuckler mentality and with confidence made a beautiful, flowing swing. He nailed the shot five feet from the hole, made the birdie, and it kick-started him to play his best for the rest of the round.

Adopting the Swashbuckler personality is also a great way to make a major shift in how you approach the game. Many times, golfers get too self-absorbed. We're worried about every last detail of how we look, stand, and swing. We're worried about the swing plane, our elbows, and our knee flex. We're worried about the people behind us and what others think about our golf games. It is enough to make a golfer want to quit, which happens far too often.

The next time you find yourself overwhelmed by the "enormity" of golf, take a page from the Swashbuckler personality and go out and just have some fun. Let go of the analysis and calculations. This will free you up. You won't be so concerned about what you do or how you do it. Instead, you'll just play the game. You might find that you'll play some of your best golf and make a major shift in how you play the game going forward.

CHAPTER THREE

THE METHODOLOGIST

"A good golfer has the determination to win and the patience to wait for the breaks."

Gary Player

THE METHODOLOGIST has a unique rhythm and tempo to the way he or she works on the golf course. In a way, observers would describe a Methodologist as being extremely structured. These golfers do the same thing over and over again. Not only is it evident in their swing, but also in their pre-shot ritual, how they measure their distances, how they select their clubs, how they practice, how they walk and talk, and perhaps even how they get ready in the morning for a tournament.

The mind of the Methodologist works in a regimented step-by-step fashion. A precedes B which precedes C. If the process skips from A to C, things are off and the Methodologist needs to start again from A. You've probably heard of having a method to your

4

madness. This certainly holds true in describing the golfer with the Methodologist personality profile.

However, to this type of golfer, it's not madness. It's actually what feels very natural and safe. Having an established method allows these individuals to achieve a higher level of focus and concentration. Because they follow a set process, there is little room for deviation or distraction, which builds trust and confidence. Rather than resulting in boredom or lack of interest, the regimented approach accomplishes exactly the opposite for the Methodologist.

In my book *The Seven Principles of Golf: Mastering the Mental Game On and Off the Golf Course,* I emphasize the importance of creating and using a pre-shot ritual before every single shot (the Fourth Principle). The ritual creates a high level of concentration, literally on the spot. A physical trigger or cue, such as fixing your hat or tapping your club on the ground, begins the pre-shot ritual, which subconsciously raises your focus. The process that ensues continues to deepen the level of focus to the moment of impact. Every top player has a pre-shot ritual. The Methodologist takes this to the nth degree. [4]

Jim Furyk, one of the world's top golfers, has a pre-shot ritual that is exact and perfect. When I use the word "perfect," I mean

perfect for him and perfect in the sense that it is always the same. He does the same ritual before every single shot. It allows him to be consistent throughout an entire round or tournament. It becomes even more powerful under duress, such as in a major championship. His pre-shot ritual helped him handle the brutal conditions and pressure to become the 2003 U.S. Open champion.

Six-time major champion Nick Faldo is a great example of the Methodologist personality profile. He had a way about him that was, for lack of a better term, habitual. He approached every shot with the same demeanor, the same process. In fact, he even involved his caddy in the pre-shot ritual, helping him line up his shots. To the observer, this may have appeared overly rigid or regimented. However, for Nick it was a good fit.

He was known to be a workhorse, constantly evaluating and making adjustments to his swing mechanics. He practiced diligently and perhaps more than anyone in his competitive set. He had a discipline to his game. Entering the final round of the 1987 British Open, Nick knew that he faced stiff competition with several players in contention. With his regimented philosophy and method-ical approach, he played what some would describe as monoto-nous and perhaps uninteresting golf, rarely taking unnecessary risks. However, for Nick, this approach fit him and the situation perfectly. He played steady golf, hitting solid shot after solid shot until he had recorded eighteen consecutive pars, earning him the first of three British Open championships. The Method-ologist personality served Nick well, especially during this major tournament.

The Methodologist also takes a similar approach to practice. He or she most likely establishes and follows a pre-set practice schedule. Within the context of each practice session, these golfers also follow a certain process. It may begin with warming up and stretching, fol-lowed by working on specific parts of the game. For example, the

Methodologist may start by hitting ten sand wedges, followed by ten pitching wedges, followed by ten 9-irons, and so on. Rarely do Methodologists practice randomly. They have a purpose and process that helps them stay focused.

This also goes beyond golf. The Methodologist may follow a set daily schedule: wake up, work out, breakfast, practice (focusing on a particular part of his or her game or swing), lunch, nine holes, practice (focusing on a particular part of his or her game or swing), dinner, evaluation of day's practice session, planning for the next day's practice session, sleep. For Methodologists, this discipline is second nature. To them, it's not rigid or strict, but rather a very simple, comfortable, easy-to-follow way to practice, play, and live. The methodical approach gives them a way to compartmentalize. They can focus 100 percent of their energy on a set action or activity for a set period of time.

To the public eye, these people might appear overly intense and self-absorbed. They're not. They're simply following a process that helps them achieve a higher level of focus, concentration, and ultimately performance. If they don't smile or converse with others, it's not that they are being rude, but rather that they are following a discipline. It is not meant to offend or turn off. For some Methodologists, this off-putting demeanor unintentionally becomes a productive tactic in competition. While the Methodologist is focused and absorbed in his or her own game and process, his or her opponents may be distracted by the apparent level of intensity, which adversely affects their play.

For many of my clients, adopting traits and aspects of the Methodologist has proven effective. I have worked with thousands of golfers of all levels, from first-time beginners to PGA pros. I believe that everyone, no matter what their level of play, has the ability to swing the club and hit good, solid shots. However, the majority lack the discipline to do it consistently.

Inconsistency is the number one complaint in golf. One shot, you're hitting a perfect 8-iron in the middle of the fairway. The next shot, with the same club, same conditions, and seemingly same swing, you're slicing it into a lake. Or worse yet, one day you shoot your best round ever, but then you follow it up the next day with a score twenty strokes higher.

To play at a higher and more consistent level, it is useful to utilize a more methodical approach. Susan was a 14-handicapper with the potential of being a scratch player. She could hit every club in her bag. She didn't need to change her swing or equipment. What kept her from playing her best golf was indecision. All she needed was a little discipline or a methodology to be more consistent in how she played the game.

For every shot, I instructed Susan to follow two steps: (1) make a conscious, clear decision on what she wanted to achieve (e.g., I want my drive to end up at the 150-yard marker), and (2) commit to that shot 100 percent. Simple and basic. If she couldn't decide what she wanted, then she couldn't proceed with the shot. Once she expressed her desired outcome, then she could move on to step two. From her pre-shot ritual, continuing to the actual swing, if she had any doubt or indecision about her desired shot, then she had to stop and start over again.

I had her follow this process first on the driving range and then during a playing lesson on the golf course. Before every shot, I asked her what she wanted. After every shot, I asked if she was committed 100 percent. If she did not have a definitive yes for either, we knew there was room for improvement. Applying this methodical approach to each shot created a form of discipline that helped her play her best golf.

THE METHODOLOGIST

STRENGTHS

Focused

Consistent

Steady

Regimented

Resilient

WEAKNESSES

Rigid

Narrow thought process

Lacks imagination

Slow to change

SEVEN PERSONALITIES OF GOLF PROFILER

Determine if THE METHODOLOGIST *personality is your dominant personality by completing the following quiz/survey:*

	STRONGLY AGREE	AGREE	NEUTRAL	DISAGREE	STRONGLY DISAGREE
	5	4	3	2	1

1. I am a person who likes order. _____

2. I follow a set ritual or routine before every shot. _____

3. I attempt to make the same swing on every shot. _____

4. I approach each hole with a plan in mind. _____

5. I enjoy having a set schedule on and off the golf course. _____

6. I am able to block out distractions and focus on my shot. _____

7. I tend to keep my golf bag well organized. _____

8. I tend to keep to myself on the golf course. _____

9. I prefer to play my own game and not be so concerned with others. _____

10. I enjoy practicing as much as playing golf. _____

YOUR TOTAL SCORE *(add up all ten answers)* _____

| 40–50 DOMINANT PERSONALITY | 30–39 SECONDARY PERSONALITY | <30 NON-PERSONALITY |

HOW TO USE THE
METHODOLOGIST
PERSONALITY

DOMINANT PERSONALITY

If the Methodologist is your dominant personality, knowing when to use the traits is as important as knowing when not to use them. For the most part, following your step-by-step approach will be the best path to play consistently good golf.

The Methodologist personality profile is most effective in situations that may be distracting on the golf course. For example, you can easily be distracted if you become aware of how well you are playing.

I often observe Tour players who are leading a golf tournament get ahead of themselves. You can see it in their eyes as they say to themselves, "Gee, I'm playing great. Only six holes to go and I win! All I need to do is shoot pars and not screw up." What happens next? Unfortunately, many Tour players know exactly what happens. They get so distracted by the potential end result of winning that they forget about one small detail—hitting the little white ball in front of them. What transpires is painful to watch. A Tour player may hit a stray shot that leads to a bogey. Then the frustration and anger build and the level of play spirals downward. As a result, he or she sinks deeper and ends up giving the tournament away.

Applying a regimented approach to every shot can eliminate the distraction of winning a tournament or shooting your best round ever, and allow you to simply play golf. With a steady approach, you minimize extraneous thoughts and focus on each shot as an individual, isolated event.

There will be a few times when you can benefit by breaking away from your dominant personality. As a Methodologist, you rely on the same consistent approach for every shot. For the most part this is effective for you, but at times releasing the regimented approach can bring on creativity and imagination.

Some shots and situations warrant a freer, more creative style. For example, if you typically hit a pitching or sand wedge from a certain distance, but the wind is gusting, try hitting a low-flying punch shot or bump-and-run to the green. Be less regimented, less rigid.

One golfer I worked with was a true Methodologist. Jane had a deliberate way about the golf course. She was like a machine— marching out yardages, calculating shots, selecting clubs. However, it was too formulaic. At times, she missed the big picture. On a thirty- or forty-yard shot from the fairway, she would usually flop a wedge to land softly on the green close to the pin. On one particular shot when Jane was just short of the green with the pin at the back, she didn't need to attempt that flop shot. This would have been an opportune time to release the regimented Methodologist

5

approach and explore the options. She could have hit a bump-and-run, chipped it, or even putted with any of her clubs and ended up with the same or a better result.

I remember when Tiger putted out of a sand trap with a fairway wood a few years ago. [5] Everyone was shocked and surprised. It hadn't been done, or at least hadn't been viewed by the public, before. Everyone assumed that if a ball was in a greenside sand trap, then it needed to be blasted out with a sand wedge. The typical Methodologist approach would have followed suit. However, as with this example, abandoning the conventional can lead to creativity and, at times, a far better result.

SECONDARY OR NON-PERSONALITY

If the Methodologist is a secondary or non-personality for you, there will be opportune times to borrow certain traits. The best time to do so is when you are faced with uncertainty, such as with a new experience or situation on the golf course. For example, if you are playing in your first golf tournament or with a new group of players and you feel nervous and anxious, using the regimented approach of a Methodologist will help you calm down and play your best golf.

Determine a set warm-up routine or ritual that you can follow prior to the tournament. This will minimize the uncertainty of the situation and eliminate distractions. It puts you in a position to be more focused on the task, which then allows you to be more relaxed in what is a foreign situation. Perhaps you could do the following:

Pre-tournament Schedule

6:15	Wake up and get ready (have outfit selected night before)
6:30	Breakfast
7:00	Depart
7:15	Arrive at golf course (check in)

7:30	Warm up at driving range (follow preset routine—hitting different clubs)
8:00	Putt (follow preset routine—putting from different distances)
8:15	Break (restroom, water, relaxation)
8:25	Arrive at tee (select golf balls, tees, marker, glove, scorecard for round)
8:30	Tee time (warm-up swings, pre-shot ritual)

This structure is second nature to the Methodologists, as it keeps them focused and helps them maintain their comfort zone. Though it appears quite rigid, the structure can help non-Methodologists better handle pressure situations.

As mentioned, using this technique at times of uncertainty is very effective. The key is to gain and sustain a sufficient level of comfort and confidence to play your best golf. Using Methodologist traits can help you do this. If you are attempting to qualify for a team, tournament, or the PGA or LPGA Tour, applying routines or rituals throughout the round can be helpful in handling the pressure. The more you can do to create a situation that feels familiar, comfortable, and relaxed, the higher the probability of you playing your best golf.

Methodologists rarely appear flustered. They just continue doing the same thing over and over again. This serves them well. The same goes for the non-Methodologist. When faced with a difficult situation, such as playing poorly, far below your capability, go back to the everyday approach that you would follow if you were playing your best golf or a leisurely round with friends on your home course. That just might help you get back into the game.

CHAPTER FOUR

THE GAMESMAN

"Pressure is playing for ten dollars when you don't have a dime in your pocket."

Lee Trevino

THE NAME of this personality really does say it all. It's the guy or gal who walks up to the first hole talking and joking nonstop, with a golf tee sticking out of the corner of his or her mouth. Or perhaps someone who's smoking a cigar with one hand, holding a beverage in the other hand, has the golf club tucked under one arm, and somehow is telling a big fish story to his or her best buddy in Vegas on the cell phone. You get the picture.

This person is fun. Fun to watch and sometimes fun to play with—that is, unless the Gamesman suckers you into a bet that you have no business playing. These are the type of people who con their opponents into some type of game or bet. They are the most convincing salespeople. You would not want to buy a used car from this kind of person.

Many of us find ourselves playing a high-stakes game with the Gamesman, far beyond our comfort level. Somehow, he or she makes us feel comfortable and safe enough to participate, even though we don't want to bet. It may start off simply with quarter skins. Before you know it, there are so many other side bets and games being played, the stakes are well up to amounts that might exceed the green fee.

Gamesmen get away with this because they are so endearing. It's hard to find fault with a guy or a gal who seems to be having a great time. Gamesmen are usually the life of the party, the golf course being no exception. They are fun people, until money is on the line. Then the jokesters become quite serious. That's how they perform at their best. They laugh and joke before and after a shot, but for that split second when it counts, they are all business. Caveat emptor—buyer beware!

Lee Trevino is the consummate Gamesman. Not to say that he intentionally steals your money. To him, it's all fun and games. He approaches each shot as if he's on the craps table in Vegas. Not only is he trying to roll the point, he's got a dozen side bets going on at the same time. He'll bet with anyone who's willing.

It's not about the money. It's about the thrill. It's about having something at stake. Gamesmen would bet their lunch money. If there was a golf tournament in which players put up their *own* money (let's say $200,000 each) to enter, with a winner-take-all format, the Gamesman would be the first to sign up.

If you fit this personality type, you may not even realize you are different from others. That's because you draw others into your game and your style of play. It would be rare for you to go a round without some sort of action on the side. You need to create an incentive for yourself. This is an advantage for you as a Gamesman because it keeps your mind off the mechanics of golf. You have one simple goal: win the bet.

There's no time to think about shoulder turn or grip or follow-through. You've got something on the line that has nothing to do with that. Your only concern is to get the job done. It frees you up without you even knowing it. This is a great trait for anyone to borrow every now and then from the Gamesman personality profile.

Many golfers have become confused by the infinite intricacies of the golf swing. Sometimes the best thing they can do on the golf course is to become a Gamesman. Focus on the goal and hit the ball Simply—just play the *game.*

One client of mine had the potential to be a very good player, but she was bogged down by the details. Eve wanted to know every last cause and effect involved with the swing. In fact, she had seen more than a dozen instructors within the past few years, many of whom shared their version of swing theory with her. Needless to say, she was quite confused, especially when some of the instruction she received was in direct conflict with prior lessons.

I could observe her confusion as she set up to the ball. She was trying to remember everything she had been taught and then incorporate all of it into her swing. She would shift forward then backward then forward again. She would evaluate her grip and stance and fidget until she thought she was in the "right" position. As a result, she appeared extremely stiff and tight. The swing was disjointed at best.

I told her to remember back to her childhood when the kids from her neighborhood would gather to play. Playing games such as hide-and-seek or tag was so simple, yet so much fun. I asked her to bring some fun back into her golf game. Keep it simple.

When I work with juniors, as young as eighteen months, I keep it simple. Basically, I say, "There's the hole, here's the ball. Use this stick to get the ball in the hole." With this simple premise, you can see the determination in a child's eyes. They get this gritty look in their faces, some of them biting down gently on their lower lip. To them it's a game, and the point of the game is to get the ball in the hole. It doesn't matter *how* they do it; that's not part of the game. It doesn't matter if they have a big back swing or a short back swing. They don't think about grip or stance. They just swing. And you know what? They usually have fundamentally sound swings . . . without even trying.

As we worked on Eve's short game, I had her apply this child-like approach. She was getting so bogged down in where to place the ball and where to shift her weight and how to hold the club that she was a rigid robot. To clear her mind and get her to simply play golf, I finally said to her, "There's the hole, here's your ball. Do whatever it takes to get the ball in the hole." I then proceeded to hand her a driver. She said, "What!?! How am I supposed to hit a driver thirty feet? This is crazy." I responded, "Achieve your goal with what you've got. Hit the ball in the hole." After resisting some more, she finally stopped analyzing, looked at the hole, and hit the ball. It rolled right into the hole. She screamed. I can still hear it.

Games are supposed to be fun and at the same time challenging. It's the challenge of achieving a goal that makes it exciting and different every time. To me, that's what makes golf great. You know you are capable of hitting and executing shots. The challenge is to allow yourself to do it and do it with total freedom and commitment. If it's too easy, then it becomes boring and mundane. Borrow the childlike, wide-eyed approach to make the game more fun, and as a result, you just might play better.

Remember to celebrate the shot. Reinforce the success of your efforts. For many, a simple "good job" under the breath is sufficient. For others, such as Chi Chi Rodriguez, doing a saber sword dance gets them pumped up and rewards them for making the shot.

THE GAMESMAN

STRENGTHS | *Fun-loving*

Enjoys games

Goal-oriented

WEAKNESSES | *Easily distracted*

Unfocused

Does not play to potential

SEVEN PERSONALITIES OF GOLF PROFILER

Determine if THE GAMESMAN personality is your dominant personality by completing the following quiz / survey:

	STRONGLY AGREE	AGREE	NEUTRAL	DISAGREE	STRONGLY DISAGREE
	5	4	3	2	1

1. I am confident on the golf course. _____

2. I enjoy competition. _____

3. I always want to win. _____

4. I like betting on the golf course. _____

5. I become more intense as the stakes are raised. _____

6. I like pressure shots or putts. _____

7. I enjoy attempting challenging or difficult shots. _____

8. I equally enjoy playing golf with strangers or with friends. _____

9. I encourage my playing partners to bet or play a game on the golf course. _____

10. I enjoy playing when a prize is awarded for good play. _____

YOUR TOTAL SCORE *(add up all ten answers)* _____

| 40–50 DOMINANT PERSONALITY | 30–39 SECONDARY PERSONALITY | <30 NON-PERSONALITY |

HOW TO USE
THE GAMESMAN
PERSONALITY

DOMINANT PERSONALITY

If the Gamesman is your dominant personality, you will find that you are unfamiliar with any other way of playing the game. You are always looking for a bet or competition. You always see golf as a game, and games are meant to be played and won.

My recommendation is to continue playing golf with the Gamesman attitude. If you can find a group of players who equally enjoy betting and playing games like you do, that is ideal. When matched up with others who aren't into betting, I know you will try your best to get them involved in some sort of game. At the very least, even if they aren't into playing for money, a friendly gentleman's or gentlewoman's bet may just do the trick.

When your playing partners ultimately turn down betting on a game altogether, bet against, or rather for, yourself. Set goals or targets. For example, if you normally hit half of your drives in the fairway, set a goal to hit ten out of fourteen. Keep statistics on your performance. Track the percentage of fairways hit in regulation. You can also apply this to all parts of your game: the length of your drives, greens hit in regulation, sand saves, putts, and so on.

Another way to satisfy the Gamesman desire is to get involved in tournament play or competitive golf. Enter charity golf events. You will enjoy the friendly competition. There are usually "closest to the pin" and "longest drive" contests, as well as group competitions for lowest team net and gross. Oftentimes there are also individual competitions.

When at the driving range, play games rather than just hitting away bucket by bucket. A game I enjoy playing is to visualize an imaginary fairway in the driving range, with left and right boundaries. I then hit fourteen golf balls (the average number of drives used in a typical round of golf) and see how many "fairways" I can hit in regulation. Another variation is with approach shots to an imaginary green. [6] You can change the distances and targets for each of eighteen shots, just as you might experience on the golf course. See how many "greens"

6

you can hit in regulation. This is also a great game to play at the driving range with or against your buddies.

Some of the newer cutting-edge driving ranges have automated games that you can play. They have concentric collection areas about a flag (similar to a dartboard). The closer the ball lands to the hole, the more points you get. The computer automatically gives you feedback on your shots. This is a great way to bring out the Gamesman personality on the driving range.

While a person with a dominant Gamesman personality benefits from embracing that approach the majority of the time, there are a few shortcomings. At times a golfer with the Gamesman personality profile may not take the game seriously enough to reach his or her potential. I played a round of golf with a guy named Stan who was a senior-level sales executive in a Fortune 100 company. He was the guy with the cell phone permanently attached to his ear. I remember one round of golf when he was literally doing a deal, with the phone tucked under his chin, while swinging the club. Unfortunately, the shot was not his best. On the next shot, he put the client on hold, asked me to hold the phone, chopped quickly at the ball, cursed a few words, then took the phone back and continued with the deal making.

For 98 percent of the time, this method works for the Gamesman personality type. In fact, the distraction of a bet or, in Stan's case, a potential sale keeps the Gamesman from being mechanical. However, there are a few situations when it is best to turn the Gamesman personality off. I remember watching Lee Trevino during a tournament joking and talking on the tee, even as he approached the ball. However, just a split second before hitting the ball, you could see the Gamesman leave him, and the look of pure focus and concentration took over when it mattered most—at the moment of impact. Even when you are in the midst of a bet or a business deal on the golf course, make sure you shift and focus for that moment to perform at your best.

SECONDARY OR NON-PERSONALITY

Some golfers may play so poorly during a round of golf that they virtually quit trying. As a result, their level of play is far below their true ability and their enjoyment diminishes greatly. At a time like this, a golfer could benefit by adopting a trait from the Gamesman personality profile. Instead of focusing on prior performance up to that given moment, a player can raise his or her level of play and enjoyment of the game by playing a different "game" going forward.

7

If a player has played poorly relative to his or her ability on the front nine, [7] and the opportunity to post a good score for the round is all but gone, then he or she can play a different game on the back nine. Instead of stroke play (keeping score for each stroke on every hole), perhaps the golfer can play a variation of the Stableford format, which awards points for how you do on each individual hole. For example, you can assign point values as follows:

My Own Game

PERFORMANCE	POINTS
Double Eagle	50
Eagle	25
Birdie	5
Par	3
Bogey	-1
Double bogey or worse	-2

The premise of this game is to get you away from being too focused on your overall stroke score. On any given hole, any score worse than a bogey takes away a maximum of two points, so if you reach a double or worse, you can pick up and go to the next hole without further penalty.

You can change the point assignments according to your level of play. If you are a new player, then perhaps shooting a bogey is a good score. Then you can assign three points for bogeys and adjust the other point values accordingly. If you are a scratch player, then assign zero points for pars and perhaps -3 points for bogeys.

By playing a different format such as this, you may find yourself with a new, fresh purpose and intensity. As a result, you may be more relaxed, hit better shots, have more fun, and actually score better in terms of overall strokes as well.

One of my clients, named Erin, seemed to have an emotional attachment to the result of every shot, so much so that it proved detrimental to her game and her health. I took her out on the golf course and watched her play the first two holes. If a shot wasn't perfect and exactly the way she intended, she would get so upset that her stomach would literally ache.

On the third hole, I asked her to play a little game. I asked her to stop playing standard stroke play and play "Hit till you're happy." In this game, she could hit as many shots from the same place until she hit one that she liked. Then on the next shot, again she could hit as many as she desired until she was satisfied, and so on.

At first, Erin was reluctant to play this game. She thought it was cheating, but she decided to give it a try. On the tee, she hit four shots before she was happy. On the approach shot, she hit three before she was happy. After a couple holes, she began to enjoy the game. The result of a particular shot didn't matter so much anymore, since she knew she could hit another if she wanted. She had become so relaxed that she began to let go of her attachment to the outcome, and as a result, the outcome improved without her trying. By the fifth hole, Erin didn't need extra swings, as she began to hit her *first* shot exactly the way she wanted.

Many golfers become extremely nervous when playing with better players. They don't want to slow them down or adversely affect how they play or embarrass themselves. I always tell them that there are many ways to play golf and still have fun. As long as you keep up with the flow of the game during a leisurely round, you can simultaneously play a different format than your playing partners. You can play a modified scramble. For example, after hitting your tee shot, you can pick up your ball and drop it next to the best drive of the group. After your playing partner hits his or her shot, then proceed to hit your next shot from there. This way you keep pace with the group and still enjoy playing the game of golf.

Let your fellow playing partners know that you will be playing this game out of courtesy. This will help you eliminate the pressure of playing with better players and eventually lead you to feeling comfortable enough to play your own ball.

CHAPTER FIVE

THE STEADY EDDIE

"Confidence in golf means being able to concentrate on the problem at hand with no outside interference."

Tom Watson

SOLID, straightforward, reliable—the Steady Eddie is the player who gets around the golf course quietly, with little flair or fanfare. Nevertheless, he or she always seems to get the job done. This is not to say the Steady Eddie doesn't win. In fact, many of the greatest champions of all time fit this personality profile.

The Steady Eddie player never seems to experience high or low points. Nor do Steady Eddies seem to move terribly fast or slow. They are very even-paced and even-mannered. They exude calm. They're the nice guys or gals. They seem like normal, everyday people who could be your next-door neighbor. The touring professionals who fit this profile probably drive their kids to school in the morning and participate in PTSA meetings at night when they're not away at a tournament. They mow their own lawns and do their own laundry.

When they play golf, they have the same demeanor. They know their own game—their strengths and weaknesses—and know when to push and when to hold back. They are so attuned to their capabilities that they rarely attempt a shot beyond their limitations. They find a way to win by utilizing their own strengths, no matter the conditions, challenges, or situation.

Tom Watson, one of the greatest players of all time, is an example of the Steady Eddie personality. Always calm, cool, and collected, Tom played and still plays the game with a very deliberate and balanced pace and rhythm. His demeanor has served him well, as he rarely experiences emotional highs or lows during a tournament. When faced with adversity or challenges, the Steady Eddie personality rarely panics or reacts emotionally. He or she simple evaluates the situation, determines the best option, and executes.

During the 2001 PGA Championship at the Atlanta Athletic Club in Georgia, David Toms was one stroke ahead of Phil Mickelson heading into the 72nd hole. Phil had driven the ball down the middle, while David hit his drive into the first cut of rough of the 490-yard par-4 18th hole. Knowing that Phil was in a great position for his approach shot and most likely would have a birdie opportunity, many players would have gone for the green to match their opponent. However, David decided that attempting a shot with the ball in the rough well above his feet and over a lake on the last hole of a major championship was not the best choice or his best opportunity to win the championship. To the audible dismay of the gallery, he elected to lay up. The moment he selected his wedge, the crowd moaned. They felt he was chickening out. They wanted to see him risk all by going for the green.

The Steady Eddie golfer often ignores the opinion of others and selects the most comfortable, high-percentage shot he or she can execute under the given circumstances. While Phil hit the green with a 6-iron and two-putted for par, David punched out to ninety yards and then hit his third shot to the middle of the green. He needed to sink his twelve-foot putt for par to win the championship. He sized up the putt, stepped up with a confident look, put a perfect roll on the ball, and watched it fall into the cup. He won the PGA Championship, not by doing what others wanted, but by sticking to his steady and consistent style.

The Steady Eddie personality profile is very appealing in team competitions such as the Ryder Cup or Solheim Cup. For these competitions, the team captain must select several two-person teams to play against opponents in alternate shot and best (four) ball formats. In addition, each player must play head-to-head against an opposing player in a match play format on the final day.

The dynamics of team competition are very different from typical medal or stroke-play tournaments. In team competitions, it is quite common to see some of the greatest individual golfers of all time perform poorly. The format creates a different kind of pressure. The reaction of the crowd, as well as the status and outcome of other matches, has a strong mental and emotional impact on one's performance. Some golfers thrive, while others falter under these conditions.

The Steady Eddie personality is usually able to ignore the challenges of said situations and play solid golf. He or she inherently plays with fewer emotional fluctuations than others, which leads to better performance under pressure. A Ryder or Solheim Cup captain can confidently and assuredly put a Steady Eddie anywhere in the lineup. He or she won't complain or react. He or she will just go out and get the job done.

At my golf academy, I can always spot the players with the Steady Eddie personality. They are very cordial and friendly and at the same time focused and secure within themselves. They aren't so concerned with what others think or do; however, at the same time, they want people to play as well as they can.

One client, named Joe, approached each and every shot the same way. However, what really demonstrated his Steady Eddie personality was how he responded to the outcome of every shot. Whether a pull, push, top, or perfect shot, he had the same exact reaction, or rather, lack of reaction. Instead of responding negatively or positively to the result, he simply observed the shot, watched it take flight, land, bounce, and roll to a stop. He evaluated the shot quietly in his mind, paused, and then proceeded to the next ball, repeating the same steady-paced pre-shot ritual. He did the same thing on the golf course—hit the shot, observed, evaluated, and moved on.

Golfers with this personality are not emotionless. They just express themselves differently, perhaps celebrating internally. In general, they are more balanced and experience fewer emotional ups and downs on the golf course.

There may be times, however, when a situation on the golf course warrants the Steady Eddie personality going outside his or her normal disposition. This type of golfer rarely takes risks, and in certain situations, this outlook prevents a player from playing his or her best golf.

At first glance, a client of mine named Andy seemed not to care much about golf. After he hit a ball, he would show little response. Even if the shot was perfect and the ball ended up at his target, he expressed little emotion. Though he did not show things outwardly, he *did* care very much about his game. In fact, he was one of the most passionate golfers I have ever coached.

In a playing lesson, his Steady Eddie personality was quite evident. Steady on the tee, steady in the fairway, steady on the green. He hit the middle of the fairway and the middle of the green. He shot par after par. He played solid golf, but his evenness seemed to be holding him back from elevating his game to his true potential. He rarely hit high-risk shots that could offer higher rewards. We discussed this.

Andy felt that the potential reward was often not worth the risk. He was happy with pars. I asked how he would feel if he went for the pin, rather than the middle of the green, on every approach shot. For the first time, I saw some emotion in his expression. He had the look of a deer in headlights. "That would make me too nervous! I could get into a lot of trouble," he said.

I then described a scenario in which he was the exact distance (135 yards) to the flag such where he could hit his favorite club (pitching wedge) from a flat lie to a green that had no hazards or traps. I asked him if he would then be comfortable shooting for the pin. He nodded yes. I told him that in order to take his game to the next level and play to his full potential, he would have to break out of the Steady Eddie approach every now and then. That didn't mean taking unnecessarily risky shots. However, when an opportunity arose to shoot for the hole in a high-percentage situation as described, then he must, in the words of Harvey Penick, "Take dead aim."

During the ensuing nine holes, Andy continued with his steady approach. However, there were two clear-cut opportunities to be more aggressive. He was in a good position to hit one of his "scoring" clubs. I told him that these are birdie holes. He shifted his mentality and went directly for the pin. Each shot landed within ten feet of the hole, giving him excellent birdie attempts, which he proceeded to make. By going outside his typical Steady Eddie personality, Andy was able to take his game to the next level.

Steady Eddie players may be complacent and satisfied with the status quo rather than pushing themselves to reach their true potential. They may be so comfortable with the way things are going that they get stuck at a certain level. If they explore the possibilities, they may realize that they can up-level their game without sacrificing their steady approach.

It can be as simple as setting a new goal. If you have a respectable 12 handicap/index, set your goals for the single digits and, more specifically, choose a number to shoot for, such as 7. Then continue playing the way you normally play. You may find a simple mind-set shift is all that is needed to play at that higher level.

THE STEADY EDDIE

STRENGTHS

Stable

Confident

Patient

Reliable

Balanced

WEAKNESSES

Status quo

Monotonous

Risk averse

Underachiever

SEVEN PERSONALITIES OF GOLF PROFILER

Determine if THE STEADY EDDIE *personality is your dominant personality by completing the following quiz / survey:*

	STRONGLY AGREE	AGREE	NEUTRAL	DISAGREE	STRONGLY DISAGREE
	5	4	3	2	1

1. I am patient on the golf course. _____

2. I am not a flashy golfer. _____

3. I maintain a consistent ritual or routine before every shot. _____

4. I am rarely emotional or distraught on the golf course. _____

5. I keep a steady focus throughout a round of golf. _____

6. I rarely force shots; rather I allow them to happen. _____

7. I generally practice and play in silence. _____

8. I could easily practice the same shot over and over until it is perfected. _____

9. I often follow a set practice regimen. _____

10. I get along with others. _____

YOUR TOTAL SCORE *(add up all ten answers)* _____

| 40–50 DOMINANT PERSONALITY | 30–39 SECONDARY PERSONALITY | <30 NON-PERSONALITY |

THE STEADY EDDIE

DOMINANT PERSONALITY

If you are a player with a dominant Steady Eddie personality, you will perform well even when the pace of play varies greatly. For example, during a slow five-and-a-half round of golf, you can apply your usual, deliberate approach rather than getting frustrated by the arrhythmic pace of play. Vice versa, if you are playing in a fast group or if the group behind you is pushing forward, you can speed up your pace between shots and then return to your optimal, even-paced speed of play for your shot.

By maintaining a philosophy of patience and keeping a long-run outlook, you can minimize emotional highs and lows during a round of golf. As a result, if you have a poor hole or stretch of holes, you can continue to move forward, knowing that if you stay the course, it will eventually lead to better shots and scores. The quiet confidence of being a Steady Eddie will minimize the possibility of panic and poor decision making. Ultimately, applying this approach will often even out the game and potentially get the Steady Eddie back into form.

There are a few times, however, when downplaying the Steady Eddie personality is necessary to achieve higher goals. For example, in the 1993 Masters tournament, Chip Beck was three strokes behind Bernhard Langer heading to the par-5 15th hole. He hit his drive to a spot 236 yards from the hole. As many golfers know, the 15th hole is a classic Alister MacKenzie risk-reward hole, with a large lake guarding the green. For the risk-taker, successfully going for the green in two can lead to a rewarding eagle. However, a ball in the water can easily lead to a bogey or worse.

8

The typical Steady Eddie personality profile would lay up and then hit a short-iron to the green with the intention of getting it close to the pin for birdie. However, in the situation described above, Chip needed to make a major move to challenge for the championship. Chip needed eagle or at least the chance at eagle to put the pressure on. This was a situation when stepping outside the Steady Eddie approach and adopting a more aggressive, go-for-it attitude was needed. He did not. He ultimately decided to lay up on his second shot. He then hit his third shot off the back of the green and got up-and-down for par—not enough to put pressure on Bernhard. It was never close after that. Bernhard birdied the 15th, extended his lead to four shots, and went on to win the Masters.

If you're a Steady Eddie, you should predetermine a few situations when it would be comfortable and appropriate to shift to a more aggressive line. For example, determine which, if any, par-3s at your home course warrant a direct shot at the pin. For that hole, adopt a trait from the Intimidator or Swashbuckler personality and go for it. [8] You don't have to do this for every shot, just for the few opportune situations that may arise. With this philosophy, the risk is still kept low, while the potential reward is much greater. You will see a major shift in your performance overall.

SECONDARY OR NON-PERSONALITY

If the Steady Eddie is your secondary personality, there are times when this approach will definitely help you play better. Once a year, aspiring Tour players compete in qualification tournaments (affectionately know as Q-School) to gain admission into their respective Tours, such as the PGA, LPGA, and Champions tours. There are a finite number of spots available through this process.

Q-School consists of several tiers of qualification. At each stage, if you play well enough to finish in one of the specified spots available, you're on to the next level of qualification. You either make the cut or you go home. The final stage of PGA Q-School is six rounds long. For this "tournament" it would be wise to adopt the Steady Eddie approach. Endurance and mental stability are essential to make it through. By keeping a big-picture outlook and a steady approach, a player can stay focused and maintain a higher level of play throughout. Too many emotional highs and lows can easily lead a player off track.

For example, even though you may shoot a great first round, if you get too excited and ahead of yourself, you might lose focus on the next round and shoot a high score. Similarly, if you play poorly early on, you must let go of that round and focus on playing the next round shot by shot. By applying the Steady Eddie approach, you play with a long-term view. This will lead to more consistent play by helping you minimize dramatic shifts that may adversely affect your game. It will bring you back when you hit a lull and keep you focused on the present when you hit a high. This will improve your overall performance.

One of my clients, named Jordan, was preparing to take the

Playing Ability Test (P.A.T.) for the second time. Any person who wants to become a PGA or LPGA professional at a golf course or country club must pass the P.A.T. to gain entry into either of these two respective training programs. This usually involves playing two rounds of golf in one day and shooting a collective score totaling no more than 15 strokes above the course rating. For example, if the course rating is 70.0, then for two rounds the total number of strokes is 140. When the player adds up his or her scores for the two rounds, the total must be no more than 155 (or 15 strokes over the course rating). For example, the player must shoot rounds no worse than 77 and 78, or any combination that totals 155 strokes, to pass the test.

In preparation for the test, Jordan worked diligently on all parts of his game: driver, fairway woods, long irons, short irons, wedges, chipping, sand shots, and putting. On any given day, he could easily shoot in the low 70s. However, several months earlier, when he took the P.A.T. for the first time, he'd shot two rounds in the mid to upper 80s. Physically, he was capable of shooting in the 70s, but his nerves got the best of him.

The first time he took the P.A.T., he got into some trouble during the first round and shot double bogey on two holes. He got so angry and emotional that it affected him for the rest of the day. He couldn't settle down. He kept dwelling on those two double bogeys and continued to play at a level far below his capability. However, what he didn't realize was that if he'd played the rest of the holes as he usually plays, he could have easily passed.

While it was important to work on his swing for the second P.A.T. and learn how to execute all the many shots required to shoot two rounds in the 70s, it was clear that the one part of his game that was missing was mental focus. When I worked with him, I taught him how to apply the Steady Eddie personality at critical moments when he felt his game wasn't perfect and, more important, when he felt his temper flaring. This proved paramount during the test.

During the first round, he hit a drive out of bounds on the third hole. His normal knee-jerk response would have been to bang his driver on the ground, tee up the next ball quickly, and try to make up for the last shot by swinging harder. However, Jordan borrowed the Steady Eddie personality and realized that it was just one of 150 or so shots during the day. All he needed to do was to settle down and move on to the next shot. He stopped, walked to his cart, and put his driver back into his golf bag. After taking a deep breath, he started his entire ritual all over. He selected his driver again, walked up to the tee slowly, and hit his best drive of the day. He went on to easily pass the P.A.T. and is on his way to becoming a PGA professional.

Borrowing traits from the Steady Eddie personality can help when things don't seem to be going well on the golf course. When a shot goes astray or if you have a bad hole or if you find yourself playing below your ability, be patient and adopt the Steady Eddie personality. If you can maintain a stable approach and outlook, then your patience will pay off. Think of a sailboat in ever changing conditions. Sometimes the situation may be calm, other times there may be a slight shift of the wind, and on occasion a big gust may come out of the blue. The best advice is to continue moving forward, making gradual and steady course corrections until you end up at your destination. This philosophy will also help you stay on track and play consistent golf to reach your goal.

If you tend to have a more aggressive nature, there will be situations when the Steady Eddie personality can level out your game. The key is to know when to use it, just as Jordan did. Another example is if you are in the deep rough too far to reach the green. Put away the 3 wood and borrow the Steady Eddie personality. If you can lay up to a spot in the fairway that will set you up to hit

9

your favorite iron to the green, you can still save your par. [9] Keep your focus on the big picture and realize that your game will even out. You do not always have to go for it, especially when the shot is beyond your capabilities. Play smart and play for the long run.

CHAPTER SIX

THE LAID-BACK

"To play well you must feel tranquil and at peace."

Harry Vardon

THE LAID-BACK personality walks down the fairway seemingly without a worry in the world. These golfers appear as if they are on a nature walk in the forest or on a stroll down the beach. This easygoing style carries into how they play golf. The swing is just as smooth and relaxed.

I enjoy watching this type of golfer, because it shows me that I don't need to be overly intense or driven to perform well. In fact, many of us can benefit by borrowing traits from the Laid-Back personality.

Fred Couples is the classic example of the Laid-Back personality. When you see Freddie walking down the fairway, he seems so relaxed. He never seems to be in a rush. Nothing seems to fluster

him. It's always the same approach—relaxed, comfortable, and easy-going. Even if he has to pick up the pace of play or get more aggressive, he never appears to be flustered. This attitude permeates his swing and his course management strategy.

Fred's swing is as Laid-Back as his personality. It's smooth, rhythmic, and balanced. You rarely see him lose his balance or wobble during his swing. It's a smooth, finely tuned motion. The word "effortless" comes to mind.

The Laid-Back personality appears to have that all-elusive repeatable swing. Every time these golfers hit a shot, it's as if you are watching them on a film looping over and over again. More noticeable is that the film appears to be in slow motion. Think of one of those old-time movies flickering frame by frame. It's as if you can see each frame one by one, in sequence. [10] The timing and rhythm lead to balance and efficiency, which lead to great shots.

Most people would think that the Laid-Back personality would lead to weak, listless shots. I believe it's quite the opposite. Having a Laid-Back personality helps these golfers hit the ball better and with more consistency. This type of golfer is able to maintain this style throughout the entire round, which allows him or her to stay more relaxed. Even though Fred has a Laid-Back approach and a

10

slow-motion swing, he was and still is one of the longest hitters on tour, hence his nickname Boom Boom.

Another player who has the Laid-Back personality is Ernie Els. He's a big guy, standing six-foot-three and weighing 220 pounds, who could be playing in the NFL. In fact, he played rugby, cricket, and tennis as a kid and could have excelled in most sports. Luckily, for the golfing world, Ernie picked up a golf club, too, when he was eight years old, and we have been blessed by the opportunity to witness the "Big Easy" on the golf course. His nickname says it all—his personality and swing are all about finesse and ease.

Golfers like Fred and Ernie appear relaxed and Laid-Back even in the heat of competition. Many fans develop an affinity or liking for this type of player. A lot of people would like to see more of that Laid-Back style in their own golf games and, perhaps, in their own lifestyles off the golf course as well.

I believe that many people are more relaxed when they hang around others who are relaxed. There's always that one person at work or school or in your club that's forever sitting back without a worry. It's as if he or she is simply *being*. Without that person trying, his or her presence makes others relax and feel at ease.

On the golf course, many golfers enjoy playing with the Laid-Back personality player. The relaxed attitude and approach serves as an example or model for others in the group to follow. By simply being in the presence of a relaxed person, golfers easily find their own relaxed rhythm and timing, in their swing and how they carry themselves about the golf course.

Many instructors advise their students to seek a model swing to emulate. I would alter that slightly and encourage you to seek a model *personality profile* to emulate. For the majority of golfers, who allow their emotions to get the best of them at times, emulating the happy-go-lucky style of the Laid-Back personality profile will help minimize errors and miscues.

When you feel as if you might erupt with anger or frustration, think of the relaxed style of a Fred Couples or Ernie Els. This might help settle you down just enough to pause and make a better decision in regards to your shot selection.

For example, let's imagine that you just sliced a drive into the rough. You're angry and ask yourself, "How in the world could I have missed the widest fairway on the golf course?" Your knee-jerk response is to attempt a shot that will make up for the poor drive.

Without conscious thought, you automatically grab your 3-wood and attempt a 240-yard shot over a lake into the wind. You say to yourself, "I need to hit this club to reach the green. I've hit it this far before. With such a horrible drive, this is my only choice." What happens next? People tend to make rash decisions and engage in careless behavior when they have a frazzled state of mind.

At moments like this, borrowing a trait from the Laid-Back profile will help. A Laid-Back player will still be disappointed with such a shot, but that player's relaxed attitude will help him or her recover faster than most others. The Laid-Back player moves on to the next shot, rather than dwelling on the past.

Richard had been playing the game of golf for four years and developed skills to potentially play well on any given day. However, his overall performance was still erratic, as his scores ranged anywhere from 78 to 102. He was baffled as to how he could experience such a wide range of scores.

Richard had a nice swing and didn't appear to have any major weaknesses or holes in his game. The only thing that was off at times was his temper. I noticed that on the driving range when he hit a shot that was unsatisfactory, without pause he would set up another ball and swing immediately. If it was another imperfect shot, he'd repeat the same hurried process. After a few poor shots in a row, he was all worked up and totally frustrated. Accordingly, his grip and his muscles were all tight and his swing had all but disappeared. I asked him if he knew what was happening to him during these times. He said, "All I know is I'm not hitting the ball very well and it's basically pissing me off!" I acknowledged his feelings and then proceeded to break down the situation.

His perfectionist approach had helped him get to his current level, but now it was hindering his overall performance and growth to the next level. If a shot wasn't perfect, he would get very emotional. He couldn't let go of those emotions, which then adversely affected the ensuing shot, and so on.

I told him whenever he felt he was close to his boiling point, to adopt a more Laid-Back mentality. If he felt like he was going to explode with anger and emotion, he should imagine a stoplight turning yellow and slow down. Take in a deep breath and exhale slowly. Step back and regroup. Take a few casual steps down the fairway to get back into a more relaxed rhythm. By adopting the Laid-Back personality profile, Richard had a new tool to help him let go of shots and get back on track with his game.

Adopting a Laid-Back personality trait, such as pausing for a moment and taking a deep breath, will help you mentally let go of the prior shot. You can then shift your energy toward making the next shot your best possible, no matter what the circumstance. With a clear, relaxed mind, you will most likely make better decisions. You may choose a wiser, more strategic route to the hole. And as a result, you will swing with greater confidence and commitment. More importantly, applying a Laid-Back personality trait at moments of crisis will get you back on track for a hole, eliminating a big number on your scorecard.

Some might mistake a person with the Laid-Back personality profile for someone who doesn't care. Not true. This personality profile does care. They are not indifferent. They want to play their best. The only difference is that they realize that their best path to success is the relaxed way.

THE LAID-BACK

STRENGTHS

Relaxed

Easygoing

Even-keeled

Unemotional

WEAKNESSES

Passive

Satisfied with status quo

Lack of killer instinct

SEVEN PERSONALITIES OF GOLF PROFILER

Determine if THE LAID-BACK personality is your dominant personality by completing the following quiz/survey:

	STRONGLY AGREE	AGREE	NEUTRAL	DISAGREE	STRONGLY DISAGREE
	5	4	3	2	1

1. I am an easygoing person. _____

2. I feel my swing is free flowing. _____

3. I feel relaxed and at ease on the golf course. _____

4. I rarely feel rushed on or off the golf course. _____

5. I feel like I'm in my own space when playing a shot. _____

6. I play my own style of golf despite how my playing partners approach the game. _____

7. I feel my best shots occur when my swing feels effortless. _____

8. I take time to enjoy the experience of being on the golf course. _____

9. I stay relatively calm and peaceful on the golf course. _____

10. I enjoy playing golf by myself as much as I do with others. _____

YOUR TOTAL SCORE *(add up all ten answers)* _____

40–50 DOMINANT PERSONALITY | 30–39 SECONDARY PERSONALITY | <30 NON-PERSONALITY

HOW TO USE
THE LAID-BACK
PERSONALITY

DOMINANT PERSONALITY

If you have a dominant Laid-Back personality profile, there are many ways to effectively apply your style on the golf course. The best time to utilize the Laid-Back approach is when you are in a situation that makes you feel intimidated, self-conscious, or pressured.

If you are playing with someone who is more aggressive and/or boisterous, do not succumb to playing his or her style of golf. If you feel pressured to enter a bet or play a competitive game, simply say "no thanks" and move on. It's your choice and you need not explain. Move forward and play your own game.

Likewise, if you are playing golf with a person who is very intense and serious, try not to adopt his or her philosophy as your own. Continue playing with your Laid-Back style. Remind yourself that you play your best when you maintain a relaxed approach. If your playing partner gets visibly upset and vocal, observe his or her behavior objectively. In other words, recognize that player's actions and antics, but do not judge and, more important, do not adopt his or her feelings as your own. That would be an ineffective use of your energy. Simply move on to your shot with your usual level of relaxation and calm.

Oftentimes, golfers are outwardly emotional when they hit a good shot or make a critical putt. Some players use a loud scream, the raising of the fist, or even a direct gesture toward another player as a competitive tactic to intimidate or distract their opponents. They may do this to increase spectator reaction and noise so that other players on the golf course can hear it, thereby distracting them and affecting how they play.

If your playing partner or a competitor does something like this, simply use your Laid-Back personality profile to deflect it. Be objective and recognize what just happened. Express little emotion for or against it. Then move on to the most important thing that concerns you—your next shot. This technique is very powerful in eliminating extraneous distractions so that you can concentrate on the only thing you have control over—your own game.

Another time to utilize the Laid-Back personality is when you feel pressure. Perhaps you are playing in a tournament with spectators for the first time, such as in a pro-am. Take a little pressure off yourself by maintaining your natural Laid-Back approach. Remind yourself that all you need to do is simply play golf. There may be many distractions that you typically do not experience, so keep your relaxed style and attitude throughout. This will help you focus on hitting shots as if you are playing the course by yourself with no one else around. Remind yourself that technically it's still you and the golf course.

There will also be situations when the Laid-Back personality profile can be a detriment. A Laid-Back approach can sometimes produce mediocre results. On occasion, adopting a more intense approach can take your game to the next level. If you are too lackadaisical, you may go on automatic pilot and play far below your ability. You may cruise through a round and not even realize that you accepted poor shots and scores.

If you face a challenging stretch of holes, perhaps the most difficult holes on the golf course, or if you are in a critical stage of a competitive round of golf or tournament, turn up your intensity, while maintaining a level of calm. Adopt what I call *relaxed intensity*. This is the complex balance of maintaining your normal level of relaxation while heightening your concentration and focus. In sports, it can be described as getting "in the zone." It's becoming hyperaware of your surroundings and the environment, which then forces you to focus deeper on the task at hand.

When I am writing a magazine article or book (including this one), rather than sitting in a quiet office, I often go to a busy, noisy coffee shop. Many people ask, "How can you concentrate under those circumstances?" I find that when I'm in a busy setting, such as a coffee shop with a lot of commotion and distractions, I am forced to intensify and increase my focus and concentration. I acknowledge the existence of distractions and allow them to continue about me, but at the same time I increase my focus on the task at hand.

11

Professional athletes, artists, actors, and performers apply this technique regularly. They are often in settings with numerous distractions: an opponent, the crowd, the noise, the lights, the camera, the pressure of the situation. Yet, when in the zone, athletes and performers describe their experiences as if they enter a vacuum and everything about them blurs or moves in slow motion. They shift into another state. Even though scientists say it is impossible to see much detail of an object moving at ninety miles per hour, baseball players explain that they can somehow see the seams of the baseball. This is an example of what I call *effortless effort.*

So those with the Laid-Back personality should tweak their relaxed approach when faced with distractions or challenging situations on the golf course. A technique that I like to use is to imagine a relative playing area surrounding myself, the ball, and the hole. [11] I imagine myself inside this area as if it is a bubble, with every thing else outside this area blurring.

Those who do not have a dominant Laid-Back personality can benefit by regularly practicing a few Laid-Back personality traits on the golf course. If you find yourself in an abyss, playing the worst golf possible, give yourself a break. Don't take the game too seriously and use a "get out of jail free" card. Don't be so hard on yourself. Set yourself free and become a Laid-Back golfer.

Shift your outlook. Keep things in perspective. One of the scenarios I often paint for my clients is to realize that if you are swinging a golf club on a golf course, in comparison to the crazy things that are happening in the world we live in today, no matter how poorly you may be playing . . . your life is *good!* And more than likely, it's a lot better than just good. If you remember this when your golf game is in the doldrums, it may be all you need to relax, take the edge off, and let your game come back. Remember, you are *playing a game.*

Apply this technique when you feel out of sorts or uncomfortable on the golf course. Discomfort may be a sign that you are not playing with your natural dominant personality. Adopt the Laid-Back personality profile for a short period of time to snap out of a funk. Perhaps for one hole, back off from trying too hard and play more relaxed and easygoing. Get out of the cart and take a nice leisurely stroll down the fairway. I always remind my students to observe their surroundings and notice the natural setting and beauty. I personally enjoy the aesthetic aspects of course design and layout. This takes me out of my intense, self-imposed box and frees me up to enjoy the game more. This usually leads to more relaxed shots, lower scores, and more fun.

One couple, Brian and Patricia, took a half-day clinic at my academy a couple years ago, immediately played a round of golf afterward, and told me that they each cut a few strokes off their regular scores—satisfactory but not necessarily spectacular. A few months later, they e-mailed me and said that they had just played in a couples tournament at their golf club back home. They also mentioned that they had played in many tournaments before, but never seemed to play well enough to be competitive. They always allowed the pressure of the tournament to get the best of them. This time, however, by applying the principles they learned at the golf clinic and adopting a more Laid-Back approach, they were not only competitive, but they won the entire tournament! In addition, they won their own respective men's and ladies' competitions the following week.

Another time to apply the Laid-Back personality profile is when you may be on your way to setting a new personal best score. Oftentimes when I am playing golf, I notice that many players begin adding up their score long before they finish the round, usually around the 13th or 14th hole.

One of my friends, Joe, did this just the other day. He was playing one of his best rounds ever. He seemed quite impressed with his score as we reached the 14th hole. In fact, the excited but nervous look on his face indicated that he was on his way to breaking his personal best score. I imagine his internal dialogue may have been as follows: "Wow, I'm playing great. All I need to do is shoot two over on these last four holes and I'll shoot my best score ever! Just two bogeys and two pars."

Unfortunately, he got ahead of himself and focused on the end score rather than playing golf and hitting the ball in front of him. His body language changed dramatically. Prior to adding up his score, he was relaxed and confident, hitting solid shot after solid shot. Now his smooth, rhythmic swing became tense and rigid as he sliced his tee shot into the trees. From there on, it got worse and worse as he shot himself out of the round. He self-destructed and ended up shooting seven over on the last four holes.

In a situation like this, a golfer can adopt the Laid-Back style to relieve the tension. I told Joe that if he was ever in a similar situation again, to think of a professional athlete, golfer, or even a fictitious character in a movie who exudes calm and relaxation. As mentioned earlier, Ernie Els or Fred Couples are great examples.

You can also think of a situation that relaxes you. Joe does a lot of things to maintain his health such as stretching, working out, and getting regular bodywork. I told him if he should find himself feeling nervous and doubtful whether he can finish a round strongly or shoot his best score, to remove himself from the situation for a moment. He should step back, stop thinking about golf, take a deep breath, and bring up those feelings of calm that he has experienced elsewhere. He could even think about one of his many trips to Hawaii, when he's at his favorite spot in a hammock under the palm trees. [12] A brief retreat of the mind can relieve stress and eliminate attachment to outcome. Then you can shift your full attention back to the present and play the next shot.

This approach also helps when golfers feel they are playing far above their expectations. Many of my clients tell me of instances when they are playing so well that they begin to question and doubt their performance. They are almost expecting themselves to self-destruct. The thought process might sound like this: "I've just shot five pars in a row. I don't normally do this. I shouldn't be playing so well.

When is this going to end? This can't last." We all know what happens next—self-sabotage and, for most, a self-fulfilling prophecy. The golfer downplays his or her performance and regresses. To elevate your game to a higher level, you must be able to break through such psychological barriers.

There are key moments to borrow the Laid-Back style. When tension and negativity arise, the Laid-Back approach will help you decrease your intensity, eliminate the pressure, and get back to enjoying the game of golf. It will free you up to make better swings and, ultimately, play your best golf.

CHAPTER SEVEN

THE ARTIST

"I build confidence when I practice a variety of shots—hitting it high or low, working the ball. A lot of golfers go to the range and just hit full shots. That doesn't build on-course confidence, because you won't always hit full shots out there. My confidence is built on knowing I can effectively work the ball in any circumstance."

JoAnne Carter

WATCHING the Artist personality profile on the golf course is like watching someone creating a masterpiece. An Artist is in a space of his or her own. Shots are created rather than hit. When faced with an approach shot to the green, Artists see so many different options. They can go low; they can go high. They can punch it; they can spin it. They can go right to left or left to right. They can bounce it off a mound and let it curve and trickle into the hole. They create whatever they *feel*.

If you have every watched a painter or sculptor at work, you know that these artists appear oblivious to their surroundings. They become totally engrossed and engaged in their work. It's as if they are in another dimension. Some artists describe the feeling of being one and the same as the piece they are creating.

For the artist, work is in some ways an exercise of *letting go*. For artists to truly reflect and express their creativity, they think less and feel more. Because they eliminate distractions and the mechanics of their actions, creativity flows more freely. At times, after a work session, an artist may finally stand back to observe his or her work, only to see it physically for the first time.

For the observer, the actions of an Artist on the golf course can be mesmerizing. These golfers glide and flow. It's as if the golf course is a canvas and their clubs are the brushes. They do not follow a textbook approach. Instead, they seem to be writing their own book. They do whatever they feel will create the end results they desire.

When they find themselves stuck in a difficult situation, they simply create a way out. Perhaps they are behind a tree and have to hit a shot under the branches, but with enough energy to reach the green, which is surrounded by sand traps. For some, this shot may be daunting, but to the Artist personality profile, it's just an opportunity to be creative.

You can see it in their body language. They always have a "can do" look on their faces. When I think of the Artist personality profile, I think of Seve Ballesteros. He was a true artist on the golf course. No two shots were ever the same. Each shot, each round, each tournament was a new canvas, and you never knew what to expect.

The aspect of Seve's game that I found most enjoyable was when he got into challenging situations, rather than in the middle of the fairway. He often found himself off in the trees or behind an obstacle. No problem. He didn't look weary, concerned, or uncertain. You could see his creative mind at work, devising a shot. Rather than giving up, he would walk up with confidence and a gleam in his eye and pull off some of the most amazing shots.

Some golfers might see one or two options for a shot. I had the feeling that Seve saw an infinite number of possibilities. As he flipped through all the options in his mind, he would ultimately choose the one that felt best to him at the moment. With a vivid imagination, he would visualize the shot from start to finish, step up with total trust and commitment, and let the Artist within create it.

He wasn't thinking about mechanics or exact distances. He was simply feeling or sensing the shot. Once he knew what he wanted, he chose the appropriate tool (just like a painter chooses the appropriate paintbrush) and let the shot unfold.

A great way to become an Artist on the golf course is to play golf or practice at the driving range when the wind is gusting. At times like this, your normal shot-making decisions no longer apply. If you have a crosswind blowing thirty miles per hour from left to right, you need to be creative in how you devise your shot. I played a round of golf under such conditions on the Big Island of Hawaii a few years ago. On this particular day, the trade winds were in full force. The wind was so severe, I had to scream nearly at the top of my lungs to communicate with my playing partner.

Under the conditions described, I first aimed down the left side of the hole toward the lava fields, in an attempt to land the ball in the fairway. With my normal swing, the ball started straight, but the wind blew it literally across the fairway and into the lava on the opposite side of where I originally aimed. If I had continued to hit my regular shot, it would have been a very long day.

I had to get creative and become an Artist. For the next shot, I visualized hitting a draw or even a slight hook into the wind. I selected my target and, with total commitment, let it go. The draw

offset the wind and ended up landing at my target in the middle of the fairway. [13]

On the next shot, going in the opposite direction, the wind was blowing right-to-left. In my mind, I took out a paintbrush and painted a cut or fade that would offset the wind. [14] That shot was pure.

13

14

What I found out was that the tough conditions forced me to be creative. Once I created a shot that I wanted to hit, I felt a strong commitment to it. As a result, my body executed the shot. To date, that was probably one of my best days of ball-striking ever.

Borrow from the Artist personality profile to put some creativity into your game. I had one client, named Mark, who was a single-digit player, but lapses of concentration kept him from being the best player he could be. I took him out for a playing lesson to observe how he handled himself on the golf course. On the widest fairway on the course, he stepped up to the tee and let loose. The ball proceeded to drift right and bounce out of bounds. He had a look of shock and disbelief. He responded in frustration, "That's why I can't break seventy. I always hit a couple of stupid shots like that."

I asked him specifically, "What did you want on that shot? Where did you want your ball to end up? Tell me the exact spot on the fairway you targeted."

"Uh, well, I figured that the fairway was so wide, I could just swing away and it would end up somewhere out there," he said.

"That's exactly what you ended up with—a shot that ended up somewhere out there."

On shots that are seemingly routine, become an Artist. Instead of hitting without thought or playing on autopilot, imagine that the hole is lined with trees creating a narrow corridor. Then visualize the shot you need to end up at your specific target in the fairway. Visualize as many paths as possible that could get your ball to the same spot. Then choose the path that feels like the best approach for you at the moment.

THE ARTIST

STRENGTHS

Creative

Passionate

Feel-oriented

Fearless

Imaginative

WEAKNESSES

Too loose

Unstructured

Dreamer

Unrealistic

Isolated

SEVEN PERSONALITIES OF GOLF PROFILER

Determine if THE ARTIST personality is your dominant personality by completing the following quiz/survey:

	STRONGLY AGREE	AGREE	NEUTRAL	DISAGREE	STRONGLY DISAGREE
	5	4	3	2	1

1. I enjoy trying new things. _____

2. I enjoy playing in all types of conditions. _____

3. I entertain several options for every shot. _____

4. I embrace difficult shots as an opportunity to try something new and different. _____

5. I get a thrill out of hitting a shot out of the ordinary. _____

6. I find ways to enjoy golf even on a "boring" golf course. _____

7. I see the game of golf as an opportunity to be creative. _____

8. I realize that there are an infinite number of ways to play the game of golf. _____

9. I see the golf course as a work of art. _____

10. I am a fan of golf course design and architecture. _____

YOUR TOTAL SCORE *(add up all ten answers)* _____

40–50 DOMINANT PERSONALITY | 30–39 SECONDARY PERSONALITY | <30 NON-PERSONALITY

HOW TO USE
THE ARTIST
PERSONALITY

DOMINANT PERSONALITY

The Artist is best when he or she is playing without limitations or confines. If this is your dominant personality, always remember to approach each shot with creativity and imagination. It is most effective when you are playing a course that others may find extremely difficult or extremely mundane.

There are some golf courses that have been designed to intimidate and distract golfers into making poor decisions. Optical illusions, strategic placement of hazards, and tempting green structures often delude golfers into attempting risky shots beyond their capabilities. As an Artist, always view all of the options available to accomplish your goal. Rather than being distracted by the illusions and traps of the hole, admire the beauty of its design and visualize a shot that will work with the given contours of the hole to achieve your goal.

Imagine you are looking at a picture of the hole and drawing all the possible paths to the hole with dotted lines. [15] There are an infinite number of possibilities, and as the Artist, you get to explore and exhaust all of them. After you've seen all the possibilities, one will rise above the rest. Then you can devise your shot and choose the tool or club to make it happen.

This same technique works when you play a seemingly boring, straightforward course. It may not have aesthetic beauty or strategic design, but as an Artist you can use your personality to inject imagination into your shots. Instead of swinging away to a wide-open fairway, design a shot that has purpose and direction. Perhaps a high fade or low draw, or you can punch it just for the sake of hitting

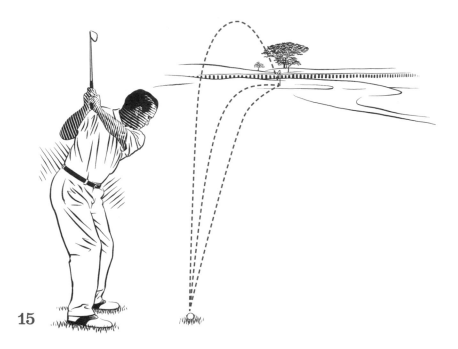

15

a different type of shot. The more variety and imagination you can apply to your game, the more fun you will have and ultimately the better golf you will play.

There will be certain situations when your Artist personality profile is not optimal. If you are in need of a score no more than a par or bogey and the hole is straightforward, going with your most confident shot, with the highest probability of success, may be the best alternative. If you are playing with a partner and your team needs to put pressure on your opponents, simply hitting the fairway or green may be all that is needed, rather than attempting to draw a drive over the corner of a dogleg. If you are in trouble in the rough or trees, creating a shot to escape through a foot-square opening may not be the best choice, even though it tempts your artistic nature.

I remember playing a friendly best-ball match with my family in Arizona when I was still a beginner. It was my brother and our uncle against me and another uncle. On the 17th hole, I hit my ball onto the fringe or apron of the green, which was about three feet wide and tightly cut. The hole was about five feet onto the green. The Artist took over, and I imagined hitting a delicate chip shot landing just an inch onto the green then rolling left-to-right into the hole. As I took out my lob wedge to hit the shot, my uncle said, "Don't get all fancy. Just putt the ball in the hole." I switched to my putter and nailed it. Stepping back and seeing the simplicity of the shot led me to playing a shot that was more appropriate given the situation.

SECONDARY OR NON-PERSONALITY

Many golfers have become highly automated on the golf course. At my golf academy, the markers and flags in the driving range do not have yardages written on them, which is the way I prefer it. One of the first questions people ask me is "How far is that marker?" I never tell them. If I do, they use a formula to determine which club to hit (e.g., 150 yards equals 7-iron, 100 yards equals pitching wedge). If you do this for every shot, soon you will lose all your creativity. You will lose all your imagination.

Be sure to bring out the Artist to hit out-of-the-ordinary shots. Try to hit a shot fifty yards with your "normal" club for that distance. Then with the same club, hit it twenty yards shorter and then twenty yards longer. Get creative. Take it high on one shot and low on the next. Bounce one in and hit one on the fly. Don't always take the standard, conventional route.

Try variations of this exercise. Pick another target fifty to a hundred yards away. Then hit different types of shots with different clubs to get the ball to the same target. Use your imagination and creativity. Think about all the options you have. Hit all your clubs and see if you can create a shot that gets you to your target. Have fun with this exercise. Become an Artist and paint any shot you desire.

If you practice this on the range, it will give you a broader, more diverse set of shots that you will be able to hit on the golf course. You will find that you have many more options than you used to have to achieve your desired goal. This will be even more useful when you find yourself in an unfamiliar or difficult situation on the golf course. You will always be able to create a shot.

On a playing lesson with a client named Mary, I dropped a ball behind some trees and told her to hit it out. At first, she looked surprised, then she was amused, and then finally she got a little angry. "Come on! Why do you want me to hit this shot? That's not fair!" she said. I told her that if she ends up in the woods, there is no manual to tell her how to get out. She has to use her imagination to create a shot that will help her not only get out of trouble, but perhaps hit a shot that she never thought she would be capable of achieving.

I told her to look at all the options.

She said, "I could hit it low with a five-iron and bounce it in the fairway and run it up to the hole."

"What else?" I asked.

"I could take a pitching wedge and hit it over the trees," she responded.

"What else?" I pushed.

"I could punch it out sideways to the fairway," she said.

I asked for more specifics. "To what exact spot?"

"Well, my favorite club is my pitching wedge, which I hit from about one hundred fifteen yards, so to that distance," she said.

"Be more specific. Pick the exact spot in the fairway that you want to approach the hole. So if the pin is tucked in the back right, then you want to approach the green from the left side of the green. Other options?" I continued.

She came up with a total of five different ways to hit her next shot. Remember there are always options. You are never trapped with no way out. Use your imagination and become an Artist to create your shots. Mary chose the option that was most comfortable and went on to save par.

To encourage creativity, always imagine at least two options for every shot. This is a great way to develop an inventive outlook when you are on the golf course. By pushing yourself to consider more than one path, you will always be developing your creative side. This will serve you well overall. Many times, golfers become so rigid in their thinking that they automatically hit their shots the same way every time, even when another option may be the best way to accomplish the same goal.

For example, if you normally hit a wedge high into the air for a hundred-yard shot, that same approach might not work if a twenty-five-mile-per-hour wind is in your face. In this situation, you must consider options: taking more club and swinging normally, punching a shot low under the wind, or hitting a low bump-and-run grounder, for example.

Applying this same concept to a shot when you encounter ideal conditions is equally powerful. Even in perfect conditions, when your wedge is the "perfect" club for a hundred-yard shot, still explore the options. You might find that hitting a different type of shot or taking a unique approach will lead to the same, if not a better, result. I enjoy links-style golf, when you often hit low shots that roll all the way to the hole. Try that sometime. This type of creative thinking will enhance your shot-making arsenal, which will prove useful in how you ultimately perform on the golf course.

SOME CLOSING THOUGHTS

"The greatest thing about tomorrow is, I will be better than I am today."

Tiger Woods

THE SEVEN Personalities of Golf are a collection of different styles and approaches to the game of golf. The goal of this book is to help people understand how one's personality or natural disposition can help and at times hinder one's performance on the golf course. It is also designed to help you utilize traits from secondary personalities to develop a balanced, well-rounded game.

When I ask my clients to describe themselves or their personality "on the golf course," I usually hear words like "aggressive," "laid-back," "fun," "tense," "nervous," "hurried," "competitive," or "relaxed." It seems that most people have a good idea of who they are and how they act on the golf course. What most people don't realize is that this can be an advantage or a detriment, depending on the situation. There are times when it may be best to downplay it and other times when it's good to strongly apply who you are.

After reading this book and taking the Seven Personalities of Golf Profilers, you may find that you have one dominant personality. I find this to be the case for the majority of people. By being aware of your dominant personality, you will better identify your natural tendencies and learn how to leverage them more effectively on the golf course. Once you begin to understand who you are and how you respond and perform on the golf course in different situations, you can then begin to learn how to maximize your strengths and minimize your weaknesses to perform at your best.

Some may ask, "Why not use your dominant personality all the time? Shouldn't you be yourself all the time?" I believe that balance is the most important factor in determining your level of success in golf. The best players usually have a great all-around game. They may have one or two areas of their game in which they naturally excel more than in others. For example, some golfers are particularly gifted with their drivers. It is the natural strength in their game. However, there are situations when the long ball is a detriment, perhaps when playing a tight tree-lined hole that requires precision. Then it is useful to downplay one's natural strength (the driver) and opt to hit a shot for position rather than distance. At other times, the hole or situation may be optimal to let loose and go for broke.

If this type of player relied solely on the long game, he or she would reach a limit in performance. If you have a great game off the tee but three-putt every other green, you will not be playing your best golf. If you can hit greens with your short irons, but rarely get that chance because you rarely hit a fairway off the tee, that will most likely lead to less than optimal results.

The top players have their natural strengths, but they also have a level of skill or at the very least proficiency in all other parts of their game in order to achieve their overall goals. As mentioned, many players today are known for their long game. However, I can't think of a successful golfer today who doesn't have a great short game to go with it. You must develop all parts of your game to succeed. The first step toward achieving balance is to better understand yourself and your golfing personality.

Each and every one of us has a dominant personality. You may like it, you may not. That's irrelevant. The point is to realize that every personality has its strengths, weaknesses, and shortcomings. To play your best, you need to know when to use your dominant personality, when to downplay it, and when to borrow from other personalities to fill in the gaps.

Identify your dominant personality and learn how to leverage the strengths of that personality on the golf course. No matter your individual style or personality, there are ways to use it effectively. In fact, most players will utilize their dominant personality for the majority of the time on the golf course. However, there will always be a few times when your dominant personality becomes a liability. That's when it's most important to stop and shift gears. It may be as simple as downplaying your typical approach or strategy for just one shot.

Some situations may warrant your abandoning your dominant personality altogether and adopting another. If your dominant Steady Eddie personality is keeping you in a rut or in the doldrums, you can adopt a more assertive personality to pick up your pace and rhythm and get your energy flowing again. Then you can return to your Steady Eddie style for the remainder of the round.

Many of my clients tell me that they want to be like a certain Tour professional golfer. I always ask, "Why?" The answers I hear include "I want her smooth, relaxed swing" or "I like how he attacks every pin" or "I just like the way she plays—steady and focused." I believe these answers reflect people's desire to express traits that they already possess, but which they have not given themselves the opportunity to demonstrate on a regular basis.

I believe that each of us carries traits from all seven personalities to a certain degree. In other words, we hold parts of all seven personalities in our arsenal even though we may not express them regularly. The key is to learn when and how to borrow certain traits from each personality to help you achieve balance in your game and maximize performance overall.

The Seven Personalities of Golf is a book to help you learn how to better manage your inner or mental game on the golf course. If you are better able to manage your emotions throughout an entire round or tournament, then you will make better decisions, hit more consistent shots, and ultimately shoot better scores. By discovering your natural style or personality, you will begin to play golf to your individual strengths, while borrowing other traits at key moments to develop an all-around, balanced game. And always keep in mind that in golf and life, balance is everything.

DARRIN GEE'S SEVEN PERSONALITIES

PERSONALITY PROFILE	PROFESSIONAL GOLFERS	STRENGTHS	WEAKNESSES
The Intimidator	Tiger Woods Jack Nicklaus Annika Sorenstam Ben Hogan	High level of focus Steady Goal-driven Wants to play best always Blocks out distractions easily	Rigid Slow to adapt Tries too hard Difficult to maintain high level of intensity Lack of emotional balance Overly intense
The Swashbuckler	Arnold Palmer Phil Mickelson Greg Norman Babe Zaharias	Fun, easygoing attitude Never bored Creative Fearless Risk-seeking	Lack of perspective Excessive Zones out
The Methodologist	Nick Faldo Jim Furyk Karrie Webb	Focused Consistent Steady Regimented Resilient	Rigid Narrow thought process Lacks imagination Slow to change
The Gamesman	Lee Trevino Chi Chi Rodriguez Payne Stewart Walter Hagen	Fun-loving Enjoys games Goal-oriented	Easily distracted Unfocused Does not play to potential

DOMINANT PERSONALITY		SECONDARY PERSONALITY
WHEN TO USE	WHEN NOT TO USE	WHEN TO USE
Competition and tournaments Games Match play	Feeling pressure beyond comfort level Constantly during several days of competition	Game at low point Fatigued Low intensity Need to put pressure on competitor(s)
Tournaments Practice rounds On the range	When an aggressive approach is unnecessary to perform well overall	Too many swing thoughts Need to make a move to win Game in doldrums
Under pressure Distracted Getting ahead of oneself	Too formulaic Overanalyzing	First-tee jitters New situations Nervous or tense from distractions
Games and bets Competition On the range	Too lackadaisical Overly distracted	Upset with score or performance Emotional or angry Intimidated by other golfers

》》》

DARRIN GEE'S SEVEN PERSONALITIES

PERSONALITY PROFILE	PROFESSIONAL GOLFERS	STRENGTHS	WEAKNESSES
The Steady Eddie	Tom Watson David Toms Byron Nelson	Stable Confident Patient Reliable Balanced	Status quo Monotonous Risk averse Underachiever
The Laid-Back	Ernie Els Fred Couples Peter Jacobson Laura Davies	Relaxed Easy-going Even-keeled Unemotional	Passive Satisfied with status quo Lack of killer instinct
The Artist	Seve Ballesteros Nancy Lopez	Creative Passionate Feel-oriented Fearless Imaginative	Too loose Unstructured Dreamer Unrealistic Isolated

DOMINANT PERSONALITY		SECONDARY PERSONALITY
WHEN TO USE	WHEN NOT TO USE	WHEN TO USE
High pressure situations Team competition Playing poorly	Situation when it is necessary to take a risk to be competitive or win	Overly aggressive Multi-round tournaments Playing below norm
Under pressure Feeling impatient Playing with intense or outwardly emotional golfers	When you shift into auto-pilot Indifferent in competition	Analysis paralysis Low points during round Distracted by playing "above" norm or expectations
On mundane or uninteresting golf courses Inclement weather Shots from off the fairway	Periodically during team competition If shot required is straightforward	Inclement weather Too automated or regimented Bored

ACKNOWLEDGMENTS

I would like to thank the many people who have been supportive and helpful during the writing of this book. Many thanks to my literary agent Ann Rittenberg, whose enthusiastic guidance and advice has helped me take a concept and create a guide for others to follow. To Keith Witmer, you have once again given life to the concepts through your gift as an artist and illustrator—it is always a delight to work with you. To Pamela Geismar, thank you for creating a book design that is both classic and modern and will last a lifetime.

To Jennifer Levesque, Executive Editor at Stewart, Tabori & Chang, thank you for your great energy—you have always been so supportive and enthusiastic throughout the entire process. To Claire Greenspan, Publicity Director at Stewart, Tabori & Chang, thank you for all your genius in sharing my work with others—it is always fun and exciting to work with you. Thanks to Michael Jacobs, Abrams President & CEO, Leslie Stoker, Publisher of Stewart, Tabori & Chang, and everyone at Abrams/Stewart, Tabori & Chang for teaming up with me again in sharing the Spirit of Golf with golfers around the world. I appreciate all your support.

To Noa Galdeira, Director of Golf at Big Island Country Club, you have been a great friend and partner to me and the Spirit of Golf Academy for many years—*mahalo!* To Jim Jacobs, thanks for the friendship . . . and your photography skills. To my brother-in-law, Lawrence Hsu, who has always been supportive, thank you for all your energy and creativity in designing everything! To my children, Maya and Eric, thank you for your smiles and laughter and always keeping me on my toes. And to my wife, Darien, thanks for always being there for me—you are my best friend, advisor, and confidante.

DARRIN GEE'S SPIRIT OF GOLF ACADEMY

As a special thank you for buying this book, we would like to offer you our exclusive bonus reports, "Darrin Gee's Top 5 Mental Golf Tricks" and "Darrin Gee's Top 10 Secrets to a Great Golf Game" absolutely FREE. Visit www.darringee.com to register.

Take your game to the next level with Darrin Gee's two-volume DVD set, *Mastering the Mental Game of Golf.* Learn the Seven Principles of Golf, his revolutionary mental game approach, with exercises specifically designed to help you play your best golf.

An engaging and entertaining speaker, Darrin is available to motivate and inspire your group to reach their potential and achieve peak performance in all aspects of life, including professional careers and personal growth.

Join us at Darrin Gee's Spirit of Golf Academy, the premier golf school in the country focusing on the mental game, located at top resorts and golf courses on the Big Island of Hawaii. On a limited basis, Darrin and his Spirit of Golf Academy program are available for corporate groups, organizations, and golf clubs at locations of choice in the United States and internationally.

To order the DVD or for more information, please contact us at:

Darrin Gee's Spirit of Golf Academy
P.O. Box 6886
Kohala Coast, Island of Hawaii 96743

Website: www.darringee.com
Email: info@darringee.com

Reservations (808) 887-6800
Toll-free (866) GOLF-433
Facsimile (808) 887-2893

ABOUT
THE SEVEN PRINCIPLES OF GOLF

Harvey Penick's Little Red Book Meets
The Seven Habits of Highly Effective People!

The Seven Principles of Golf: Mastering the Mental Game On and Off the Golf Course offers Gee's simple yet profoundly powerful mental and inner approach to golf mastery. Proven successful by golfers of all levels, including PGA Tour professionals, at Gee's Spirit of Golf Academy, his Seven Principles of Golf blend timeless concepts into a dynamic and effective step-by-step process leading to better shots, lower scores, and more fun.

More than a coach or a sports psychologist, Gee is a true philosopher of golf—and of life. His method embraces a golfer's total performance, applying the same principles taught in golf to personal and professional life. In presenting techniques for quieting the mind, enhancing awareness, visualizing each shot, developing pre-shot rituals, and finding one's natural swing, Gee prescribes a series of exercises to be performed on and off the golf course.

The Seven Principles of Golf exercises are beautifully illustrated by Keith Witmer and the book is cloth-bound with a ribbon marker. *The Seven Principles of Golf* was the third-ranked golf title in the Northeastern United States and has been published in several languages worldwide. Available at all major bookstores, independent booksellers, and online at www.darringee.com.

ABOUT THE AUTHOR

Darrin Gee is the author of the book *The Seven Principles of Golf: Mastering the Mental Game On and Off the Golf Course* and founder of Darrin Gee's Spirit of Golf Academy, headquartered on the Big Island of Hawaii.

He has received national recognition as a leading authority on mental and inner golf mastery, and has been credited for growing the game of golf. His mental game techniques have helped thousands improve their golf games. The Seven Principles of Golf have been adapted to help people achieve peak performance off the golf course in their professional and personal lives.

With a background that includes corporate strategy, management consulting, marketing, and sales for major Fortune 500 corporations, Darrin is a sought-after motivational speaker at corporate meetings, incentives, and conventions. He is a consultant and advisor to executives, companies, and organizations.

Darrin received his MBA from Northwestern University and holds a BA in psychology from UCLA. Darrin lives on the Big Island of Hawaii with his wife and fellow author, Darien Hsu Gee, and their children, Maya and Eric.